Railway Ghosts

by J. A. Brooks

Jarrold Colour Publications, Norwich

ISBN 0–7117–0285–3
© 1987 Jarrold Colour Publications
Printed and published in Great Britain by Jarrold and Sons Ltd,
Norwich. 287

Contents

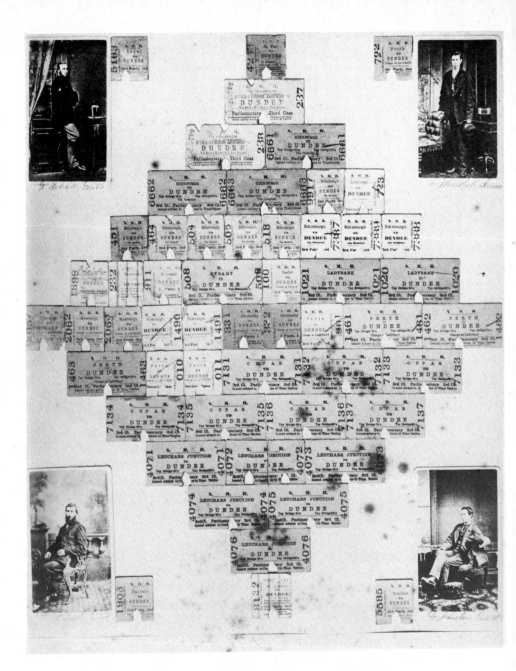

Macabre Mementoes: 'These tickets were collected at St Fort Station, on 28 December 1879, by Robert Morris, Agent; Wm. Friend, Ticket Collector: and Alex. Inglis, Porter, from the Passengers who lost their lives by the Fall of the Tay Bridge.'

Preface

I foresee what the effect will be – it will set all the world a-gadding. Twenty miles an hour! why, you will not be able to keep an apprentice boy at work; every Saturday evening he must take a trip to spend the Sabbath with his sweetheart. Grave plodding citizens will be flying about like comets. All local attractions will be at an end. It will encourage flightiness of the intellect. Veracious people will turn into the most immeasurable liars; all their conceptions will be exaggerated by their magnificent notions of distance. And then, there will be barrels of pork, and cargoes of flour, and chaldrons of coals, and even lead and whisky, and such like sober things, that have always been used to sober travelling, whisking along like a set of sky rockets! It will upset the gravity of the nation! Think of flying for debt; a set of bailiffs mounted on bomb-shells would not overtake an absconding debtor, only give him a fair start. I go for beasts of burthen, it is more primitive and scriptural, and suits a moral and religious people better. None of your hop-skip and jump whimsies for me.

Written by an opponent of the railways in 1836.

We are pained to state that a labourer, who was working in the excavation of the railroad, at Edgehill, where the tunnel is intended to come out and join the surface of the ground, was killed on Monday last. The poor fellow was in the act of undermining a heavy load of clay, fourteen or fifteen feet high, when the mass fell upon him, and literally crushed his bowels out of his body.

Liverpool Mercury, 10 August 1827. The first recorded death of a railway-worker.

THE GREAT WESTERN RAILWAY.
BY
J.C.BOURNE.

Introduction

Strange, that there should be such a shortage of authentic railway ghosts. When this title was suggested I innocently believed that research would uncover a host of colourful hauntings, but I was quickly disappointed, and although railwaymen would sometimes hint at certain 'spooky' locations, invariably there was no explanation for their unease.

Neither have railways inspired many memorable fictional ghost stories (Dickens's *The Signalman* being the classic exception). The late Sir John Betjeman's *South Kentish Town* appears for the first time in print here; although hardly a ghost story the terror of the timid commuter trapped in a deserted station is very real, and the piece has a flavour that could only have come from the pen of the late Poet Laureate. He read it on the BBC Home Service more than thirty years ago.

Many of the stories here are based on real locations and events, though some liberties have been taken. Thus readers may notice inaccuracies, most of which (I hope) are deliberate, intended to enhance the telling of the story. However, none of the characters are based on real people, living or dead.

Perhaps these tales will stimulate the memories of those connected with railways to recall other stories of the supernatural based on personal experience. Few industries have such a potential for ghostly activity: it would be a shame to lose its folklore and legends when so much of its worldly ephemera has been preserved.

An early railway disaster, Thorpe-next-Norwich, 10 September 1874

The Sword in the Sky

Humphrey's heart sank as he first set eyes on his new batch of 'punters'. They shuffled down the steps from the Stratocruiser at Prestwick flexing stiffened muscles and taking deep breaths of fresh Scottish air, splendidly colourful in an array of clothing as tasteless as any that their courier had yet encountered. He motioned his photographer forward as he introduced himself:

'Can I trouble you for just one tiny moment, please, ladies and gentlemen. Let me introduce myself: I am Humphrey Sutherland-Ross, your guide for the next twenty days. First, may we get the photograph taken: you know that you're celebrities here.'

Having let the other passengers disembark the photographer began arranging the group on the aircraft steps. There were seventeen of them altogether, many of the men clad in the garish tartan jackets which Humphrey particularly abhorred. Two of the ladies unfurled a banner which read 'The Ghost Hunters' Club of New Jersey – Scottish Convention, 1955.'

Over the couple of years that he had been involved with parties such as this, Humphrey had become skilled at concealing his true emotions. He now exuded the bonhomie of the British upper class. His native accent was totally suppressed (twenty-eight years before he had been christened Albert Spraggs in a chapel at Stepney) and with a professional eye he ran his eyes over the women of the party, looking for the ones who would cause him trouble. Invariably these would be of early middle age, either divorced or separated from their families for this brief vacation. They would be intent on having as much adventure as possible in the short time available, and inevitably the courier would be the initial target, especially when, as in the case of Humphrey, he was young and personable. Two of them, he noticed, stole predatory glances at him, while a languid young man was fluttering long eyelashes. Though Humphrey's sexual inclinations were cosmopolitan, to say the least, so far he had been successful in avoiding approaches from his clients. He was uncertain whether this abstinence helped to make his work easier or more difficult.

The first hurdle in the trip was their passage through customs and immigration. Humphrey's carefully nursed friendship with Alastair Cameron, the senior customs officer (whom he privately regarded as a bewhiskered bore) ensured that the weird Spiritual Signal Amplifier was imported without question, likewise their expensive cameras and tape-recorders. They were soon installed on the coach which was to take them to a luxury hotel close to the airport. Humphrey looked forward to an easy evening knowing that many, fatigued by the long journey, would retire to bed before dinner. Quickly and efficiently they were allocated their rooms at the hotel. A briefing was arranged for the next morning at half past nine, after breakfast.

Humphrey had been responsible for many such groups. He was a partner in Go Places Exclusive Tours (U.K.), Inc., a company which tailored holidays in Britain around the interests of the groups who approached them. The tours were always very expensive, and often catered for those who enjoyed staying with titled hosts in crumbling castles and stately homes. The special interests more usually embraced history or antiques: this was only the second Ghost Trip that Humphrey had conducted, and in this case the Secretary of the Ghost Hunters had insisted that their tour should be exclusively in Scotland since so many of the members had Scottish, or at least Celtic, roots. Humphrey's task was made more difficult by the tour being arranged for early April, when so many of his contacts in the stately homes business were still taking their hard-earned rests in Alpine or Mediterranean retreats. However he had managed to piece together a tour of thirty ghostly locations, though in order still to please the title-hunters of the party this had to entail out-of-work actors taking the parts of noble owners in two of the venues. They were also engaged for the spectacular finale of the tour, held at one of the grandest of locations, when an after-dinner pot-pourri of Scottish ghosts was to be presented, from the Monster of Glamis to Mary Queen of Scots.

But much lay ahead before this last event. Humphrey Sutherland-Ross outlined his plans for the first week at the meeting the following morning:

'Well, ladies and gentlemen, I trust that you are now refreshed and keen to discover this lovely country's wealth of psychical phenomena. As you know, we stay here at Turnberry for a further night: those who wish for a nocturnal excursion will be taken for a watch at Hermitage Castle – the most sinister of the castles of the Border counties, and once the home of the black magician, Lord Soulis. You will remember that local inhabitants finally threw him into a cauldron of molten lead, but none the less he is still to be seen around the place with his familiar, Robin Redcap. The latter is said to hold the key to treasure hidden in the castle, so you might subsidise your costs by a visit there.

'Tomorrow we move north to explore Edinburgh. A coach has been arranged, and this will take us to a house in the Old Town which has a ghost of impeccable pedigree. It hints at unspeakable events that the family were involved in many generations ago, and thus only a few know of its appearances. We will lunch at the house and you will have the afternoon and evening to set up your apparatus and investigate the haunting.

'On Thursday we take the train to the north where I have assembled a sequence of outstanding locations. We will stay at a house said to be haunted by the ghost of Bonnie Prince Charlie himself, close to the battlefield where his army was routed by the English. From there we will visit a church with a spectral skull, and Rait Castle, which has

the sad ghost of a lovely girl whose hands were cut off by the wicked chieftain of her clan. She then leapt to her death from the ramparts where she returns, blood-stained and hand-less. I am sure that she will appeal to your ghoulish tastes.'

This concluding remark was heartfelt, as Humphrey thought secretly that ghosts, however highly born, were rather poor form, seeking to flaunt their old grievances in distasteful ways. That is, if one chose to believe in them at all, and since he had never seen one Humphrey had little respect for the enthusiasm of the punters, who regarded his hauteur as typical British upper-class reserve (the joviality he had shown when he had first met the group had soon worn thin).

As it happened the Wednesday in Edinburgh was disastrous. Not only did the ghost fail to appear but their host met them in a state of glorious drunkenness. With the haunted room darkened he made lecherous advances to the most matronly of the American ladies, and after these had been loudly rejected turned rudely on Humphrey and demanded that he should take his party of prattling idiots away.

Thus it was a fairly disgruntled group who assembled at the station the next morning for the train to Inverness. Humphrey had used his charm to persuade the authorities to stop the train at the disused platform at Culloden Moor, which was convenient for the house at which they were to stay. The Edinburgh morning was bright yet cold, but as they travelled northwards the day got progressively more gloomy, and by the time they got to Perth sleet had begun to fall from a slaty sky.

As the train began its long climb through the mountains the sleet turned to large flakes of moist snow which soon fell quickly enough to obliterate the bleak prospect of distant peaks and featureless moorland. At Aviemore they had to wait for a time to allow a snowplough to clear their track, and the next twenty miles to Culloden were travelled at very low speed.

At last the train drew up to the little platform at Culloden. Humphrey's party had been instructed to travel in the front coach of the train since the platform only extended for the length of two carriages. An attempt had been made to clear the snow, but it had been a futile battle, and the blizzard had settled more snow there ankle-deep. It was a subdued group who were left with their pile of baggage watching the train disappear into misty whiteness.

A cheerful Highland voice broke the spell:

A Train in a Drift of Snow,

'Well, ye'll not be getting through to the House for quite a time. Ye'd best come this way to the warm.'

The voice came from a burly figure in uniform – a cape covering his shoulders. Eyes of remarkable brightness twinkled beneath equally remarkable eyebrows, which projected some distance in front of the face and wore a covering of snow and embryonic icicles. He led the way to shelter, the front parlour of his railway house, where a great fire of crackling pine logs burnt, and his wife was ready with cups of tea and potato-cakes.

'Likely ye'll be here a while, now,' he said, 'so it's best you make yourselves easy. The General sent out a couple of cars for you all but they got no further than the gates of the policies. Ye'd have fared better carrying on to Inverness.'

This had crossed Humphrey's mind too – at least they would have been assured of beds for the night – but things would have turned out much worse for them but for the hospitality of Mr Mackie, who he found out to be the signalman and linesman at Culloden Moor, where the station had been closed for years.

'Of course all of you are welcome to stay here for as long as you need. I've a feeling that yon's the last train we'll see through here today, but when the snow eases you gentlemen could try walking down the track and then through the park. You have to look for the drive crossing that leads direct to the House.'

These words hinted at the course of action that he expected the menfolk to take, though he continued to be a genial host, broaching very fine 'sample' bottles of unblended Scotch from the local distillery in order to keep up their spirits. Dusk began to fall early that day, and although the clouds still kept low, the snow ceased and water droplets began to fall from trees and gutters.

'The thaw's on its way', proclaimed Mackie, 'you men should be off now if you're to get to the House yonder, and send for the ladies tomorrow: we shall care for them with comforts enough, and they'll not miss you for the one night.'

Thus the men, some with borrowed footwear, shuffled out into the gloaming. Deep snow lay between the platforms, but the exposed levels of the track beyond, towards Inverness, were relatively clear. At first Humphrey led the way, but soon his slight physique gave him an excuse to relinquish the responsibility to a burly American. About a mile from the station the track dived into a steep cutting. Here the snow had accumulated and the men were forced to climb from the level ground of the trackbed to the hillside above. Here they had their first wide view of the countryside, darkened though it was by the fall of night. Rows of young conifers extended in every direction. The unevenness of the ground between the ranks was masked by snowfall, but the stalwart American leader was not beguiled by this, even though he could see the cutting curving away to the left.

'We follow the fence,' he called to the rest of the platoon, living again his service as Master Sergeant during Patton's European campaign, and chewing an imaginary cigar butt.

Humphrey suffered most. He had a dislike for any form of physical exercise, and the deep snow and steep slopes had quickly taken toll of

LNER   WESTERN HIGHLANDS   LMS
IT'S QUICKER BY RAIL
FULL INFORMATION FROM ANY LNER OR LMS OFFICE OR AGENCY

his stamina. Yet he was the first to see the spectre. The tableau began in the sky. Clutching at a fence-pole to drag himself to the top of a particularly steep hummock his eyes rested for a moment on the dim skyline above. An enormous sword was held upraised there by a bloody fist. He shouted in terror, pointing at the apparition, and the others turned their heads in the direction of his gesture. They all saw it: he knew that instinctively, just as he sensed that it was but a prelude of terrible events to follow. The sword slashed down through the sky, revealing a scene alive with colour, light and horror.

The group forgot the discomfort of the cold as the landscape changed. The sword vanished, as did the ranks of conifers and the snow, disclosing a barren landscape all around. The waters of the Moray Firth could be seen in the distance from the high moorland on which they stood, though skeins of wind-borne sleet drifted across the sky to mask the vista. However, it was the activities in the opposite direction which claimed their attention.

The lines of battle were drawn up. The neat red-coated ranks of the Royal (English) forces faced the untidy lines of be-kilted rebels. Puffs of smoke betrayed the positions of the English cannon, and seconds later came the sound of the exploding charge – more like an iron door being slammed than a roll of thunder. Even before the sound arrived the awful effect of each shot could be seen. At first three or four men in the first rank of the Highlanders would be tossed aside – their severed limbs or halved torsos being flung high and wide by the dispassionate iron ball, which, unchecked, continued its deadly course to the lines behind. Although from a distance it seemed as though it should be possible to dodge from the slow progress of the shot there were few who could move quickly enough to avoid it, as it bounced unpredictably over the rough contours of the moor. Even beyond the second ranks the balls continued to threaten the officers in the field, the cavalry and their horses.

The remorseless artillery barrage was alien to the battle-rules of the clans who were receiving it. They clamoured to be allowed to charge, beating their targes (hand-shields) with their great swords, and running forward to shout Gaelic threats and insults at the red lines facing them. Their pipers could be heard playing the rants or pibrochs of the clan, while the drums beat out a heart-stopping, hypnotic, accompaniment.

Although in reality this scene lasted an hour or more, in the re-enactment it was over in a matter of minutes. The clansmen began their advance on the English. Seeing this the English artillery changed from using roundshot to grapeshot (charged cartridges with small leaden balls, nails, and scraps of old iron). This proved even more deadly at the shortened range, and swathes of the advancing Highlanders were mown down as they made their way through the brown heather, their kilts tied up above their thighs. Those who survived this merciless barrage were faced by the three lines of English musketry, the first crouched on one white-gaitered knee, and two further ranks standing behind, their red coats bright even through the smoke and fret of that gloomy day.

The first volley of musket-fire took terrible toll of the yelling clansmen who were advancing on the English line. It was followed by the equally deadly fusillades of the second and third ranks, yet still the rebels advanced, their faces contorted not with fear, but with frustration and anger at not being able to fight. Some came to a halt about fifteen paces from the muskets of the English, stopped by the relentless fire. For a moment they stood there helpless, for they had thrown away their small arms during the advance, waving their great claymores and axes and shouting at their enemies. Their swords continued to slash ineffectually at the air as they were mown down, until they were at last dropped, unbloodied, on the sodden ground.

A few were able to overcome the volleys of the redcoats and penetrated the first line of infantry but were stopped by the bayonets beyond. Very few English fell in the battle where the Scottish supporters of Charles Edward Stuart were slain in great numbers, one upon the other, until there were piles of bodies three deep in front of the English lines.

The final horror of the encounter was still to be revealed. The rebel advance had failed, the battle had been lost for the Prince. Those of his men who survived attempted to flee from the battlefield. The bewildered, sickened onlookers from a later age were spared no details of the gruesome slaughter which followed. The infantry were given the order to pursue the retreating rebels, which they did with ferocious, merciless, enthusiasm. Another detachment was sent to seek out the clansmen who still lay on the moor, alive but injured. Hundreds of these were slaughtered in cold blood, many being made to suffer hideous cruelties before the final pistol shot or bayonet thrust.

As night fell, and the English were called away from their butchering, so the scene faded slowly away, being replaced by the former, modern, landscape. The spell was broken, Humphrey looked at his watch and concluded that time must have stood still, for it was still only thirty minutes since they had left the warmth of Mr Mackie's hearth. It took the party a further two hours of struggling through the deep snow before they at last arrived at Culloden House, where they were welcomed by their host. There had been little discussion concerning the events they had seen: they had walked and slithered like robots, or like survivors of some dreadful accident who have suffered no injuries apart from severe shock.

The General knew intuitively that some misadventure had befallen them apart from exposure to the elements. After his guests had been shown their rooms and made comfortable he ushered Humphrey, whose face was still set and ashen, into the library.

'You'll feel the better for telling me', he said, as he poured a fiery, peaty, almost colourless whisky from a decanter. 'You saw the sword in the sky, did you not?'

LMS   INVERNESS   LNER
by NORMAN WILKINSON R.I.

He listened quietly to Humphrey as he attempted to put into words the ghastly scenes that they had witnessed. At the finish, after a moment's reflective silence, the General commented:

'Well, it's what your party paid their money for, though I suspect that the womenfolk will not feel too pleased at having missed it. My great-uncle once saw a part of it, but he would never speak of the occasion. It's remarkable, but, I understand, not as uncommon as might be supposed. I have a friend who has a place on the Welsh Borders, in Shropshire, and he has often seen a great rabble of an army on the move, camp-followers and all, though he says it is the more strange for passing by without a sound: no clank of arms, no whisper of speech. In Scotland there's said to be another ghostly army at Letham in Fife: that one is supposed to fight the Danes by the side of a loch that disappeared centuries ago. Of course you know about the Battle of Edgehill in England which took place again the following Christmas-tide on three successive nights. The King sent a general from Oxford specially to witness it, and he reported seeing his late colleagues-in-arms on the battlefield, and some of them being slain.'

The subsequent days of the ghost tour were, thankfully for Humphrey, uneventful. As the General had predicted, the ladies of the party were very disappointed at having missed the highlight of the excursion, however horrific it might have been to them. Their complaints about the lack of ghosts, for which they held Humphrey personally responsible, made him vow never to repeat the outing – his enduring wish was never to set eyes on a ghost again. Nevertheless this does not prevent him from regaling his friends and colleagues with the story from time to time. For several years now he has been a partner in a small antiques business, and lives in Sussex with his friend Patrick.

The Lullington Poster

31 December 1967

My wife Yvonne, of course, laughed at me when I first told her that I was being haunted. She used her withering tone, Beaufort Scale 10, to put me down – 'You've not enough imagination to turn off the telly, let alone see a ghost', and she resumed her contemptuous charging about the house, as though maximum disturbance meant maximum cleanliness.

Yet they had been going on for several months then, had my supernatural experiences, and I only mentioned them to give her one last chance to be nice to me, to address me without scorn, treat me as though I were a grown human, not a sub-normal ape.

I don't know how well you know the railway system of South London, but take it from me, it's boring, and seedy (which, I suppose, might be the words my wife would use to describe me). You gaze out of the window of the 7.43 in the mornings at an endless pageant of back windows, broken greenhouses, scrapyards, abbatoirs etc. until you're so depressed that when you get to London Bridge you could

Thirties style in station architecture – Tolworth, Surrey

throw yourself on the electrified track. If you're lucky, going home on the 5.37, it's dark, so you only have your own reflection to look at, and the other seedy, boring human beings who occupy the compartment with you.

I had been doing this same journey on the same train on every working day for ten years when I first noticed something different about Lullington. This was a deserted station where trains never made scheduled stops. It had been built just before the war, to a fairly posh design, as a speculator intended to develop the place into a new 'urban village', but after the war the houses were never built and the station never opened. It looked odd, for its architect had chosen the fashion of his day – ocean-liner curves and ceramic tiling – which was now all cracked and mildewed.

This particular day I was slumped in the corner seat, trying to get high on the thought that there might just for once be a presentable female who'd forgotten that the bathroom curtain was undrawn, when I saw a strange thing on Lullington platform: someone had put up a poster there. We went through too fast for me to tell who it was, but the next morning we slowed down there, and I saw clearly. It was a picture of Jayne Mansfield. Funny, that, I thought, just a portrait of her without any words, though certainly it was decorative enough. A couple or so days later I read she had been killed in a particularly nasty road crash – lost her head she did, and I thought no more of it till I saw that the poster was no longer there, nor did the wall show any trace of where it had been. About four weeks later another face appeared on the wall, a politician this time, who in much the same way, shuffled off this mortal coil within forty-eight hours.

For the rest of the year my journeys to work held a new interest to me. Lullington provided me with a forecast of several famous people who soon suffered unexpected, usually violent, deaths. When I saw their faces I was at first shocked, but soon came to accept the fates that were in store for them. After the first two or three incidents I made certain that I was the only person seeing the fatal posters. 'Oh!' I said, all innocence to my fellow passengers, 'what a strange place to put up a poster.' They couldn't have failed to notice it because the train was stopped opposite it at the time, but since they all looked at me as though I was crazy and did not comment I knew that I was the only one to see it. For some reason the poster only appeared when I was on the 7.43; if I travelled earlier or later it was never there, nor did it ever show itself in the evenings. Only once did I succumb to the

21

temptation of trying to warn the poster's victim of the fate in store for him or her – I did so to see whether my intervention could change the course of events. When I spoke to my man, a television interviewer, he treated me with such arrogance that I realised the uselessness of my phone call. I heard him say to somebody in the background 'Oh, it's just someone who says I'll die tomorrow,' as he rang off. What the person he spoke to made of the unexpected heart-attack that struck down the interviewer the next day, I'll never know.

15 July 1969

I discovered how to turn my clairvoyant poster to my own use by accident. For some weeks nothing had appeared on the station wall at Lullington and I had begun to give it a somewhat cursory glance. On this occasion I was miles away as we passed the deserted station, thinking of work and the nosy sod who had been brought in from outside and put over me. It was his face which was suddenly on the poster, and two days later a gas leak blew him heavenwards in his own kitchen. At first it shook me to realise that it was probably me who had brought about his downfall (upfall would make better sense) but then I realised the great potential of my secret weapon. I decided to have a practice run with my mother-in-law, who I reckoned to be the most interfering, vicious old cow south of the Thames. I had long thought that if it hadn't been for her my marriage might have worked, but from the first she had turned Yvonne against me. I visualised her in her curlers and apron, a King Size drooping from her ever-nagging gob, as we ran through Lullington. Surprise, surprise, she chose a novel way to die. Opening her top loader when it was still spinning fast, the ends of her scarf got caught up with the load and she was slowly smothered by her own knickers, etc., I liked the way my ghost operated.

I worked my way steadily up the promotional ladder, three of my colleagues suffering expedient deaths. Having achieved the level that I reckoned I deserved (the boss began to call me 'Jonah'), I was content to sit back and delegate – the mark of a good manager, it is said, and certainly the method leaves you plenty of time for lunchtime boozing.

Last night Yvonne cut up specially rough, coming out with her versions of home-truths which she knew I would find hurtful. No area of my life escaped her tongue, and she flounced off to sleep in the spare room announcing that to her the marriage was over, and she would get every penny off me she could. So I put her on the poster this morning, imagining her at full blast against me, clutching her flea-ridden mongrel in one hand and the mop in the other.

P.S. I am now a broken-hearted widower. At 10.31 a.m. today (17 July) Yvonne electrocuted herself with the vacuum-cleaner she had been on at me to mend for the last six months. R.I.P. Yvonne.

31 December 1977

I see that it is ten years, now, since I wrote the first account of this affair and my circumstances have certainly changed since then. Wifeless, I found my tastes were beginning to be rather too expensive for my income, and got to wondering how my ghost could make me money. I continued my journeys on the 7.43 and at intervals saw the faces of the famous at Lullington though I did not, for a time, use again the deadly power that I had at my command. The brilliance of my plan, when it came to me, was overwhelming. I began to travel First Class in company with a set of wealthy stockbrokers who always met in the First Class compartment nearest the front of the train. One by one I began to kill them off. When just two were left I took the richest one aside and told him that I had killed his travelling companions by means of witchcraft, and if he didn't buy me off he would meet with a similar fate. By way of illustration I bumped off his one remaining friend the same week. The means of their deaths made it impossible for anything to be pinned on me, and for a gent like him to go to the police and complain of being bewitched was just not on, so I felt safe in asking for an income of £20,000 a year from him. This was agreed to, but I had only received one payment when I was confronted by two heavies one night and only the unexpected passing of a copper on the beat allowed me to escape intact. The next morning I was on the train, and having been lucky enough to glimpse the faces of the heavies, was able to put them both on the poster together. They died in a car crash and their boss payed up without argument after that. This had taught me a lesson, though, and I took on my faithful bodyguard Graham, who has been my shadow ever since. To pay for this luxury, I have been forced to put the squeeze on three more wealthy gents on the 7.43. There is now a definite shortage of First Class passengers on the train, and I wonder whether I will be able to maintain my standard of living (or should it be death, ha ha!).

20 January 198–

If I still worked at my old job in the City I would have retired last year, but in fact I threw that up many years ago, when I decided that long-range death threats against the world's wealthiest families was the answer to the shortfall of the prosperous on the 7.43. I obtain pictures of the nearest and dearest of tycoons and then put the pressure on from a distance. After the deaths of a couple of their loved ones they acknowledge the power of my 'witchcraft' and pay up handsomely into my Swiss bank account. I seldom have occasion to use the 7.43 now but yesterday I did so, intending to extinguish the sister of an obstinate client. But what I saw at Lullington makes me fear that this is the last entry I will make in this account. The state of crisis between Russia and Pakistan would seem to put us closer to the holocaust than we have ever been, and yesterday, when the train slowly drew through Lullington I saw that every inch of the old station's walls was covered with faces – there must have been millions of them. Today the faces were not there, but I saw the workmen had begun demolition work on its buildings. Behold, Armageddon is at hand!

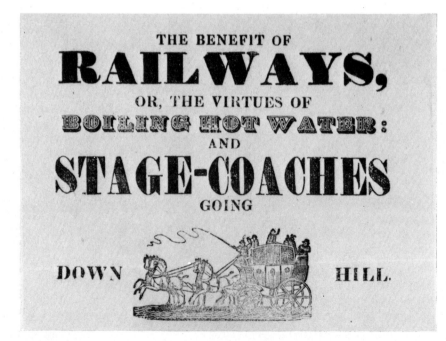

THE BENEFIT OF **RAILWAYS,** OR, THE VIRTUES OF BOILING HOT WATER: AND **STAGE-COACHES** GOING DOWN HILL.

Dead on Time

It was the moment that the Professor had been looking forward to all day. Ignoring all the textbooks and learned periodicals that lined the shelves of his study he reached for a book with a faded blue cover – the timetable for the London and North Eastern Railway for the winter of 1937. He placed this on the meticulously tidy desk, turned on the light, and opened the book at the pages dealing with the services between Edinburgh and Glasgow.

It would seem to be an unlikely pursuit for one of the world's most eminent lawyers – playing with trains. Professor Tobin enjoyed his academic life and his advice was sought by governments as well as corporations, but his delight was the elaborate model railway that he had, over many years, built in a large shed in the garden of the Victorian mansion in which he lived on the outskirts of Edinburgh.

The layout was complex. Modern electronics meant that almost any manœuvre could be undertaken. Each locomotive was fitted with

Edinburgh TRAVEL BY EAST COAST ROUTE

FULL INFORMATION FROM ANY L N E R AGENCY

a coded module which obeyed commands given it by the controller. A vast web of wires beneath the baseboard connected points, signals and uncoupling devices to the control point. It had evolved, in truth, into a railway system in miniature, though the modelling of the scenery did not relate to any real landscape. The Professor enjoyed giving his layout different identities, adapting it to suit the demands of the timetable that he had decided to follow, and choosing rolling-stock of the right period and livery.

It took the whole evening to work out the movements of the trains that were to run on the layout the next day, designated as Friday, 10 December 1937. The details were noted on large sheets of paper specially ruled up for the purpose. A meeting took care of the morning, but after lunch the Professor could look forward to an afternoon and evening of intense mental activity – what his long-suffering wife scathingly called 'playing with trains'.

The day began inauspiciously: cold and dull, and as the tedious meeting closed the sky had become so dark that lights had come on in the buses, and there was the feel of snow in the air.

The Professor had chosen two o'clock as the start of the exercise, and hoped to go through to seven. It would be a triumph if the timetable could be worked for that length of time without mishap. Only on one previous occasion had things gone perfectly to plan, when a short two-hour programme using the east-coast main line had been successful. At other times some gremlin or carelessness had intervened so that 'The Great Hand from the Sky' had been forced to come to the rescue. On these occasions the Professor had comforted himself with the thought that such events often disrupted the smooth running of real railways. Acting out the tasks of a hundred or so engine-drivers, signalmen, etc. was a severe mental strain, and Professor Tobin usually ended feeling mentally and physically drained, yet the pure fun of the thing usually outweighed the irritation of things going wrong, so he found it fairly easy to ignore the scorn of his family (perhaps he had been unfortunate in having three daughters).

The operations began with the departure of a three-coach stopping train from the eastern terminus which today served as Edinburgh Waverley. Headed by his beautiful (though unglamorous) model of a J37 0-6-0 it completed two circuits of an inner track, stopping at every station it passed, before being switched on to a branch line where it eventually reached its terminus, North Berwick. Meanwhile two other trains had been started – a northbound express parcels and a main-line express from Waverley. The latter passed out of the section quickly, so was simply driven once round the main circuit and then on to the storage tracks.

As the afternoon progressed the Professor became more and more engrossed in the procedures, which became more and more hectic as the rush-hour approached. His fingers were constantly flicking over the lever-switches which changed the signals and set the points. His eyes checked the relative positions of the trains on the tracks, while in his mind he counted the number of circuits each had completed. The movements became almost hypnotic, and several times he jolted himself out of a trance-like state in the way that one does when on the brink of sleep. A final time and he let himself succumb, but to his surprise though his fingers were now still and his hands were away from the control knobs, the trains were still running perfectly without his intervention. He occupied a God-like position high above

Windsor Lad No. 2500 fresh from the paint-shop. It was another A3 Pacific – No. 2744 Grand Parade – which was involved in the Castle Cary accident .

the layout, as the tiny trains shunted, drew out as long expresses, or busily fussed as suburban services between one station and the next.

Now, too, there was a perfection about the layout. Before, although the modelling was good, it had still been a very imperfect version of the real thing, with a multitude of blemishes and inaccuracies. These had faded way, and in the dull light of the afternoon it was possible to see smoke coming from the chimneys of the locomotives, and warm lights on in the carriages.

The landscape was now readily identifiable. A real castle stood on the crag overlooking the station, its romantic outline silhouetted against the skyline in the gathering misty gloom. A Gresley Class A3 Pacific moved grandly out of Waverley Station with a nine-coach train, diving into the tunnel below Castle Terrace to emerge, a minute or so later, at Haymarket. Instinctively the Professor knew that this must be the 4.03 p.m. Glasgow express, due to arrive there at one minute past five.

Once through Haymarket the train picked up speed. Its outline could only dimly be seen, but the glow from the firebox and the lights of its carriages made it easy to recognise, even when deep cuttings or buildings momentarily screened it from view. Then it vanished completely for almost a minute and he realised that it must have reached Falkirk Tunnel, and glancing westwards saw the lights of the town itself. At this moment the Professor felt himself whisked onwards down the line at great speed. The bewildering, kaleidoscopic effect of this ceased abruptly and he found himself much nearer to the line, looking down on a signal-box. A little beyond the box a passenger train was stopped at a small station, its end-lights glowing feebly. Hurrying towards the signal-box were two figures. He was able to see them enter the box, where wild gestures punctuated a brief conversation. This ended with one man tearing open the door, hurtling himself down the steps and on to the track. Now the Professor could see the reason for his behaviour. The Glasgow express that he had started from Waverley Station was approaching the signal-box at full speed. A quarter of a mile beyond the unguarded passenger train stood at the station waiting for the return of its fireman from the signal-box, where he had gone to make sure that the rear of his train was protected.

The Professor could see the driver at the controls of the Pacific,

Class D29 Rob Roy. *It was* Dandy Dinmont *of the same class which was hauling the Dundee train at Castle Cary*

peering out of the cab window through snow flurries which masked his vision. He saw him glance at the veranda of the signal-box where the distraught signalman frantically waved a red flag at him. Instantaneously there was the bang of the detonator laid on the track by the fireman, and sparks flew from the engine wheels as the driver pulled hard down on the brake.

The Professor saw the awful inevitability of the disaster without experiencing it. He was spared the sight of the express ploughing into the back of the Dundee–Glasgow train, its engine carrying on for a hundred yards beyond the point of impact, folding one coach neatly up on itself as though it were tinplate. At this moment a small but vital blood-vessel had given way to extinguish the Professor's consciousness as effectively as the express had obliterated the last two carriages of the train from Dundee standing at Castle Cary Station.

No coroner could speculate on the power of the psychic echoes released by the Professor's hapless choice of timetable. His body was found by his wife some hours later, sprawled across the layout, his hand on the A3 Pacific; its wheels were, by some fluke, still in contact with the track, and spun helplessly. A few inches down the track, standing at a station, was another passenger train.

The Dobwalls Sorcerer

Bill Raven had been signalman at Dobwalls for more than twenty years when the new Station Master was appointed. From the first he had prepared himself to resent the newcomer, for although good-natured he intensely disliked any changes to the pattern of his days. In his mind he expected to grow tolerant of the newcomer over the months, but it was soon apparent that this would not happen. He surprised himself by the way that his antagonism grew for he had seldom felt hatred for anyone in the way that he did now: there was nothing about Martin Cudlipp that he could ever like or admire.

Cudlipp had served as an NCO with the Irish Guards. His straight back and brusque manner spoke of the years he had spent on the parade-ground drilling recruits. He had a short haircut and thin, clipped moustache.

In contrast Bill was a large untidy man of few disciplines. Over the years his job had become moulded to his personality so that now he was accepted as one of the great 'characters' of this stretch of the Great Western. His anecdotes (and the tales told by others of his

The name of the station here is only a thin disguise!

On God's Wonderful Railway – an 0–6–0 pannier tank at Fairford

escapades) made him a favourite with railwaymen and villagers alike. He was never short of young 'helpers' in the box, who pulled off the levers and made him tea while he directed operations from the depths of an ancient armchair. Often he kept watch over the pastures to the rear of the box with a twelve-bore ready on his knees. He was particularly partial to jugged hare steeped for some days in the rough local cider. A kindly, contented man who loved a gossip (on or off duty), Bill was a favoured patron of the pub which stood close to the station.

All this met with disapproval from Martin Cudlipp. In his first week as Station Master he had made his feelings plain: no strangers in the box; no scrumpy before coming on duty; no poaching from company property, and uniform to be worn during every shift.

Bill told him to go and jump off the Liskeard Viaduct and carried on as before. His Station Master then wrote out a detailed report cataloguing all of the signalman's misdemeanours and showed it to Bill before dispatching it to the Section Office. Within a few days Bill

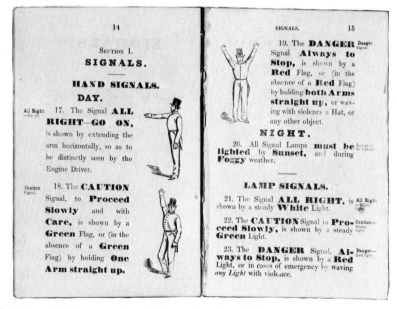

Staff demonstrating hand signals. Lancs. & Yorks. Railway, c. 1920

was visited by the Superintendent, who settled himself down in the old armchair for a long chat.

'Well, Bill, seems you've been and rubbed this new fellow up the wrong way. You'd best be careful of him, boy, he's got friends in high places. One of the officers he served with is on the Board – that's how he got the job.'

Bill pulled off the down main for the afternoon goods and grinned at his old mate. 'So that's how he came to get here when there's lots better than him, railwaymen back from the war, still on the dole.'

'Like I say, Bill', the Superintendent replied, 'it's best to be careful till you gets to know his ways. He may not turn out to be such a bad chap in the end.'

To Bill's mind that was wishful thinking; nevertheless he followed the advice by toning down his lifestyle to a degree, though he was still able to exasperate the Station Master on every occasion that they met.

Certainly, under the reign of Sergeant Cudlipp, Dobwalls Station had been transformed. Previously vegetables had been grown in the flower-beds ('Part of the War Effort' his predecessor had explained to inquiring passengers: the war had been over for seven years). Now they were planted out with neat, regimented rows of bedding plants. The hedges were clipped back with immaculate precision. All edging stones were of uniform size and whitewashed. It was the Station Master's intention to win the Best Kept Station award for Dobwalls, and to achieve this he felt that the signal-box should be made neat and tidy too, and its homely comforts thrown out.

Of course when he suggested this to Bill the latter flatly refused. He pointed out that all the signalmen on the line had their small luxuries, and no jumped-up army twiglet was going to deny them to him. And if he had thoughts of going to his friends at Head Office again, then he'd better beware, 'Us country-folk don't take kindly to that sort of meddling.'

Martin Cudlipp, incensed by this defiance, immediately sent off a further note to the Superintendent (who promptly mislaid it) complaining of being threatened with physical violence. When Bill came to hear of it, he said quietly 'I was warning him of worse than that.'

Spring in Cornwall is a delightful time of year. The trees by the lineside show a fresh green of dazzling brilliance, and a host of wild flowers garland cuttings and embankments. At this time the station

garden at Dobwalls was looking good too, and drew forth numerous compliments from pleased passengers. The Station Master's chest swelled out even further when this occurred, while Bill Raven looked on sourly. It was announced that the judges of the Best Kept Stations competition would be visiting the section during the first week of June and care of the garden was given precedence over all other business as the last days of May slipped away. The Station Master's preoccupation with the flower-beds was, perhaps, unfortunate as he tended to overlook more mundane matters. Most serious was the situation with the Honourable Daphne's Blue Persian kitten, Tabitha. This had been carefully fed and watered at the station after disembarking from the London train and seemed to be perfectly happy in its basket while it awaited the arrival of the chauffeur from the Hall who had been summoned to collect it. It was a mystery how the tin of white paint, used for platform edging and for the dazzling white stones that surrounded the flower-beds, came to be upset over the kitten's basket. No one would own up to the accident, which was the more disastrous for His Lordship being a drinking crony of the Chairman. Cudlipp was summoned to Plymouth for a stern reprimand, while Tabitha's chances of being Best of Show at the Devon disappeared for good.

Shortly afterwards came the equally puzzling incident of the lost cabin trunk. This belonged to another notable squire who sent it on in advance of his holiday in Jersey. It was last seen on the platform at Dobwalls but subsequently disappeared completely, only returning after six months. It transpired that it had travelled all the way to New Jersey. Again the Station Master was held to be responsible and his light, in the eyes of his employers, grew dim.

Bill was sympathetic to these misfortunes, and shook his head sadly, implying that they were inevitable: 'Ah, you see, he's gone upsetting the little people with his army ways.'

This sentiment was born out soon after when the local pannier tank, on the pick-up goods, driven by Bill's great mate George, inadvertently snorted a great volume of sooty water from its chimney which hit the underside of the footbridge before descending on the Station Master and his garden. It took three lads, engaged for the task at the expense of Cudlipp's own pocket, a couple of days to restore the white stones to their former pristine glory. The flowers, and the uniform that the Station Master was wearing at the time, took longer

A navvy on the Great Central

to recover. The latter knew that the event was no accident, and began to suspect that the earlier incidents were also contrived malevolently. His suspicions were reinforced the next Saturday (the judging of the station was to take place during the following week) when in the gloom of dusk he came upon Bill engaged on a strange task by one of the flower-beds. He was on his knees staring intently at two toads which were among the flowers. Strangely they were harnessed by lengths of twitch-grass to a sort of plough made of twigs.

'What the hell are you up to?' he demanded, thinking at first that his beloved flowers were being sabotaged.

'Well now, how can there be harm to you or your precious flowers in me giving my paddocks a walk?' By using the ancient name for toads the words had a sinister ring to them, and Cudlipp shivered involuntarily as he watched the signalman gravely pick up the animals.

The next day all the flowers in the beds had wilted. There was no natural reason for this that the Station Master could discover. He had watered them regularly and watched them intently for signs of parasites. At first he suspected that his enemy had used a potent weedkiller on them, but then noticed that the few weeds in the beds which had escaped his attentions still flourished. There were no flowers to greet the judges as they climbed from their special train on the Tuesday following, and it was obvious that they were sceptical about his excuses.

The affair had a terrible effect on Cudlipp. Like his flowers, he wilted. His figure, formerly imposing and upright, became spare and bent, and his manner vacant and indecisive. His eyes sank deep into shadowed sockets and he was unable to stop his hands from shaking. Seeing this, the Superintendent sent him to the company doctor, who advised rest at a convalescent home at Sidmouth.

After three weeks Cudlipp returned with much of his former spirit restored. He forsook the demands he had previously made on his staff for army-style neatness and discipline, but could not conceal his hatred for the signalman when he was forced to converse with him. For a time life at Dobwalls resumed its old style, comfortable and uneventful.

Bill Raven was content again: he began to forget about the former unpleasantness and took up all his former habits. In the signalbox he held court to his village friends: the young who delighted in opening the road to express fish and parcels trains (he never entrusted them with passenger services), and the old who came for his story-telling or wealth of experience at poaching. He was the king of his castle, and the box became an oasis of quiet when his relief, Jack Newton, began the other shift. Occasional small misfortunes continued to befall Station Master Cudlipp, and though these were comparatively trivial the villagers noticed them and began to speak of him being still under the spell.

Summer melted into a warm, golden autumn, and it would seem to have been hard to find anything other than content in Dobwall's sheltered valley. Cudlipp's accident shattered this calm.

It happened on one of the rare occasions when Bill Raven was alone in his box. The daily pick-up goods was receding into the distance when Cudlipp crossed from the siding to the platform. As he stepped over the points the signalman leaned back on the lever which controlled the road to the siding. Rotten wooden boards gave way without warning beneath the feet of the Station Master who found himself securely and painfully trapped by his ankle midway between the tracks. He shouted up at the signal-box, but Raven had busied himself pulling off the home and distant for the down *Cornish Riviera*. The sound of its whistle could be heard faintly as it passed through Liskeard. He shouted again, and the bulky figure of Bill Raven came to the veranda of the box and looked down dispassionately. Their eyes met; a gloating triumph in those of the signalman, fear and despair in the Station Master's.

'For God's sake put on the distant,' he shouted.

'Why should I do that for the likes of you,' came the reply. 'Would you, if I were there now?' His ruddy, chubby face beamed a happy smile. 'Fate's not been kind for you here, 'as 'e?'

The oncoming express could now be heard more clearly. The beat of its wheels on the joints of the rails sounded out loudly through the enclosed valley.

'You bastard, may you rot in hell. You will remember me through this.'

Raven only heard a few of the following words as the train bore down on the trapped man: the driver saw him at the last moment and threw the regulator over, applying the brakes at the same time. but this did little to check the momentum of the train. Yet the signalman heard: 'When he shall be judged, let him be condemned: and let his prayer become sin. Let his days be few; and let another take his office. . . .'

On the Severn Valley – a pannier tank hauls a winter special

Then the noise of the passing train drowned out the shouted words, and he saw a confusion of rushing carriages, brown and cream, following the polished green of the locomotive. The coaches passed, squealing to a standstill about half a mile up the track. Waving grass betrayed the place where the writhing torso of Cudlipp had been thrown, but Raven still heard the words of the Cursing Psalm even though he knew that it was impossible for a man with such terrible injuries to utter them.

'Because that he remembered not to shew mercy, but persecuted the poor and needy man, that he might even slay the broken in heart. As he loved cursing, so let it come unto him: as he delighted not in blessing, so let it be far from him.'

There is a belief in Cornwall that if a person who suffers death through injustice recites Psalm 109 just before death, the maledictions are certain to take place. It was so with Bill Raven. His end came soon, but not before much suffering.

Within a week of the torn remains of Martin Cudlipp being laid to rest the curse took effect. Nothing that Raven ate stayed down. Before he had been a man who had loved his food, but within a month he became a shadow, yellow and haggard. His former friends deserted him – they felt the aura of doom about him. Just eight weeks after the death of Cudlipp he was found hanging from the balcony of his signal-box. Jack Newton, his relief, applied for a transfer from Dobwalls a few weeks later. Soon after Bill's death he had found a small figurine of wax hidden in a cloth behind the levers. Its body was pierced by thirteen steel needles.

Gentle Geoffrey

'Nor should we forget the benefit to rural human genetics brought about by the railway: with less inter-marrying the "village idiot" has disappeared.'

I came across this sentence the other day in a book written in the early years of this century. I thought wryly that though this might be true the railway still managed to attract its share of idiots; most of them ended up in management.

Then, from a shady, remote recess of the brain a memory stirred and conjured up a face that was grotesque by reason of its lack of symmetry, and for the fawning, grinning expression it habitually wore. The face belonged to an almost equally grotesque body – hunched and dwarf-like, it had a peculiar crab-like style of movement which recalled Charles Laughton's portrayal of Quasimodo. In a moment the simpleton's name came back to me – Gentle Geoffrey, a more apt, transposed version of his real name – Geoffrey Gentle.

When Gentle Geoffrey first appeared at the shed feelings were divided as to whether he should be welcome among us or not. I was in the canteen (a grandiose name for our ramshackle mess-hut) on the occasion of his first, dramatic, visit. It was about 5.30 of a winter's afternoon. Some of us had been out putting down fog detonators, others were occupied in more routine matters – raising steam, coaling, boiler-cleaning and so on. There were about twelve of us in

Camden Shed

the hut, sipping at the scalding, coppery tea that had been on the go for the past half hour, talking nineteen to the dozen, and generally getting a warm by huddling as close to the glowing stove as possible. I was facing the door when I saw it begin to open, then it stopped and I shouted:

'Come on, whoever you are. You'll perish us by the draughts you're letting in.'

The door opened slowly a little farther, and then, with the strange sidling motion we were to know so well, Gentle Geoffrey came among us.

All conversation stopped abruptly. God had made this creature absolutely devoid of beauty or grace: instead in all of his aspects there was an all-surpassing degree of ugliness. From his earliest days he must have become used to people recoiling from him in horror. Children would run away screaming to bury their faces in their mothers' aprons. Yet it turned out that he had been greatly loved by his two elderly parents (he was their only child) and one or two of the children in his neighbourhood were protective and kind to him. However, this was not sufficient to satisfy his need for the warmth of human company, and it was this that had brought him in our midst on that cold winter's afternoon.

His entrance was timid and obsequious. He held a greasy, bedraggled cap in his hands, and seemed to be trying to speak, though he only succeeded in making animal-like grunts. Fortunately he turned out to be known to one of our men.

'Why if it isn't Gentle Geoffrey', said Barnaby (with a name like that a surname was redundant). 'He lives near us, and though he looks bloody horrid he can't help that, and there's a lot of good in him. Come on Geoffrey, have a cuppa and get yourself warm.'

The smile that lit up the distorted features had a rare warmth and candour, and he shuffled across the little hut to take a stool next to Barnaby.

'Poor bugger leads a sad life, especially since his folks passed away,' explained Barnaby. 'When he gets to know us a bit he'll be able to make himself understood – he's desperate for company, yet so shy he can't make words at first. But he'll soon come round, and he's a lovely old chap, aren't you, Geoffrey?'

Barnaby punched him lightly on the arm, and again the face twisted itself into a grin of delight. Geoffrey was pleased at finding himself accepted.

The weeks that followed must have been the happiest of Geoffrey's life. He pottered about amongst us, learning where he could be most useful and acting as a cheerful, ever-eager jack-of-all trades, albeit an unpaid one.

The majority of the men at the depot welcomed his presence there: a handful let it be known that they didn't appreciate his help. They were the ones who were unable to overlook his disfigurement, though the only unkindness they showed was the manner in which they totally ignored him. Geoffrey's hours at the shed were spent in a wide variety of ways. His main duty was to tend to the shabby, smoky rest-cabin, the canteen, and to make sure that the fire in the stove was burning bright, and the tea kettle ready. We always made sure that there was enough in our lunch-boxes to feed Geoffrey too, until one day he proudly arrived with one of his own, filled with roughly cut bread and cheese.

Coaling at Derby, 1909

His other tasks included fetching and carrying errands (to the shop for cigarettes or papers, to the stores for rags or oil) and helping with the messy business of cleaning boilers or clearing the fire-box.

Geoffrey's special friend was Jack Kirkley, the tank man. Perhaps their close friendship stemmed from the fact that both were oddities. Jack was practically a midget – he had to be for his job; crawling through the baffles of the side tanks of a small tank engine would be impossible for a man of normal stature. He had to wriggle his way as far into the tank as he could and then, returning backwards, had to drag as much of the muck with him as he could, pushing it back to Geoffrey for him to scoop into a bucket. These two became such firm friends as to be almost inseparable, even though Jack was the elder by thirty years. However their friendship only existed at work, and I once heard it said that on one occasion when Jack was in town with his wife and met Geoffrey in the street he totally ignored him.

Geoffrey's time of happiness at the shed was destined to be brief. Sadly, the place that he had come to love above everything was to turn into a hell for him from the moment when three new apprentices were taken on in the autumn of that year. Two seemed to be likeable enough lads but the third was a natural bully, and he took an instant and intense dislike to poor Geoffrey. Larry was slightly older than the other two lads and considerably bigger. In fact he was as big as any man at the depot and though a bully was far from being a coward. When two of the young cleaners attempted to 'initiate' him during his first week at the shed (the ceremony involved being 'washed' with a mixture of ash and coal dust) he laid both of them flat. At first I thought that his teasing of Geoffrey was good natured, but I soon learnt of its darker, vicious, side.

One day he stole Geoffrey's precious lunch-box and hung it from the semaphore signal just outside the 'canteen'. Geoffrey spent twenty minutes looking for it, with the new boys not bothering to conceal their mirth, before Larry pointed it out to him, just as the signal-arm dropped and the box fell, depositing its contents in the path of a pick-up goods. On several occasions Geoffrey was soaked by oily, sooty water when Larry blew off the vacuum of an engine with exquisite timing. Although Geoffrey suffered the humiliations stoically, their effect was to take away his hard-won confidence and reduce him from a happy, simple, friendly human being to his former self – a shambling, incoherent wreck.

Larry's obvious success at this transformation spurred him to even

greater efforts. Geoffrey's former eager-to-please attitude became a thing of the past, and for days on end he would desert us, preferring to roam the streets. Then he would reappear, to be teased and humiliated again by Larry, utterly without mercy. It is shameful to admit that none of his former friends, apart from Jack, stood up for him. Even Barnaby and I, after token protests at first, shrugged our shoulders and allowed Larry to get on with it. Jack, however, remained loyal and protected Geoffrey as much as he could. Being so small he was safe from any violence and possessed a sarcastic wit that often prevented further mischief.

The climax to the subtle torture came one golden afternoon in late autumn. Armed with rodding gear and a pressure hose Larry was clearing out the tubes of a very neglected B1. Having by subterfuge enticed Geoffrey on to the footplate of the locomotive, he applied the air-hose quickly to a number of the boiler tubes. The resulting deluge of ash, grease and scale half-buried poor Geoffrey.

'There, you daft bugger, let that teach you. You're not welcome round here while I'm here. You're just too bloody ugly, and if you come back I'll do for you properly, so just shove off!'

And Gentle Geoffrey, soaked and filthy, lurched away. At a little distance he turned and shook a fist, struggling to find words. But he could manage only a few painful grunts, and after a moment turned away towards the yard gates. We never saw him again, alive.

Larry's accident happened soon after. He was cleaning out the tubes of an ancient J36, rodding away, hunched up in the firebox, when somehow the fire-box door was closed on him. He quickly began to stifle in the heat retained by tubes and bricks, and then, to compound the tragedy, the water from the boiler, not far off boiling-point, was run off into the ash-pit. Larry was literally broiled alive. It took the ambulance men the best part of an afternoon to retrieve all his remains.

When it was hinted to the police that Larry might have had an enemy at the shed they immediately began to search for Geoffrey. All his usual haunts were visited but there was no sign of him, and his neighbours swore that he had not been at his house for some days.

Shortly afterwards the little J72 of the depot was towed in. Its injectors were refusing to work, even though the loco had been in for overhaul two days previously. Accordingly its side-tanks were drained, and there, wedged between the baffles, Jack found the body of his friend. At the inquest the cause of death was said to be drowning, and so the dual tragedy seemed neatly explained: Geoffrey had taken his revenge for the humiliations he had suffered at the hands of Larry, and then, terror-stricken by what he had done, had hidden in the empty side-tank, and fallen asleep there. Waking up as the tanks had been filled with water, he had been unable to extricate himself and so had died. Thus perhaps both victims had got what they deserved: Larry for giving him hell, and Geoffrey for retaliating in such a ghastly way.

If this solution was correct and just it would be expected that the souls of both parties would rest, if not comfortably, at least reasonably quietly. However, about a fortnight after the funerals Jack came rushing into the stores (where I worked at the time). His face would certainly have been white (or even ashen) had we been able to see through its layers of muck.

'I've seen him again! In the tank of that old J36. It was Geoffrey, and he just looked at me and grinned!'

Great Eastern cleaners, c. 1910

The Supervisor sent him home, reckoning that the previous macabre events (it had been Jack who had brought out Geoffrey's body) had slightly unhinged him, and he was told that he would be taken off tank-cleaning duties for a time.

The depot's belief that Geoffrey's ghost might haunt the yard was strengthened by his next appearance. One of Larry's fellow apprentices was on night shift, and having graduated to engine-cleaner was allowed to move locomotives to the coaling-stage on his own. As, seated on the driver's seat, he eased the great beast out of the shed he happened to glance across the cab. There, sitting opposite him, was Gentle Geoffrey, a serene smile on his distorted face. This at any rate was the explanation the apprentice gave for leaping off the engine, thus leaving it to run free to the main line. It became derailed at the station throat and disrupted services for most of the following day. The apprentice was sacked – not even the intervention of the

Union could save him. ('Do change your story, son, for God's sake! If you keep saying that they'll lock you up for good.')

I suppose Geoffrey had his revenge on us all, in his own way. The place became a shambles: no one wanted to be on their own for fear of seeing him. Folk claimed to have met him in the strangest places. One fireman, relieving himself in the convenience, found Geoffrey standing next to him, smiling gormlessly. A driver, glancing through the windows of a train stopped opposite, saw Geoffrey in the Dining Car, a vast breakfast before him. Management stepped in and commissioned a priest to perform an exorcism in an attempt to bring about peace at the yard, but to no avail. It took the end of the Age of Steam, and the advent of the soulless diesels, to make Geoffrey pack up. By that time most of us haᴅ moved on to downgraded jobs in other parts of the region. Looking back, I think that we all deserved to suffer retribution: perhaps it was this that finally laid poor Geoffrey's spirit to rest.

The Man in the Corner Seat

Some people are compulsive travellers and become addicted to it in the same way that gamblers or drinkers take up their vices. A few such addicts are fortunate in finding occupations that allow them freedom to indulge their needs – they become agents with far-flung territories perhaps, or ticket inspectors, or even travel-writers.

Within the ranks of the latter group the name of Hilary Gore was famous. He contributed two weekly pieces to *The Graphic* (at that time the most widely read of popular newspapers) as well as occasional, very polished, accounts of his exotic travels to the glossy monthly or bi-weekly publications read by the 'smart set'.

Hilary Gore was a restless person. There was something within him which was never satisfied, even by the most luxurious of excursions. Established in an apartment at one of Europe's finest hotels, within two days he would be chafing for pastures new. He hardly gave himself the opportunity to write down his impressions of one country or city before he was off on his travels again. However he had the uncommon talent of being able to encapsulate his impressions of a place within minutes of arriving – his eye for the ridiculous making his writing racy and amusing.

Yet often his pen would be a cruel weapon, and by the occasion of his thirtieth birthday he had made many enemies. By then he had completed his millionth mile of rail travel and to commemorate this event he produced a book (which immediately became a best-seller) entitled *Milestones*. His acquaintances (his nature and his restlessness never allowed him friends) wondered whether the world held enough places for him to visit within his lifetime.

Apart from travelling, Hilary was a man notably lacking in enthusiasms – his passions were invariably negative. Rarely did he find a place or even a dish to praise, but it mattered little for this was not the sentiment that his readers sought. They looked to him for pungent descriptions of idiotic hall porters, or the way that he could sniff out the comical from the most grandiose occasion: the slug emerging shyly from the *salade de chasse*, or the confusion of the wine waiter after he had sent back the third bottle of '93 claret.

Over the years Hilary's comments on towns, hotels, trains, boats and people became ever more acid. He positively hated finding a place too perfect for a deflating paragraph. He frequently spent hours of his

journey inventing witty remarks about his destination – which he had yet to see. A weariness came over him gradually which was reflected in his writing. He began to feel his observations to be stale and contrived; only his enthusiasm for perpetual motion never waned. On his rare visits to the office he sensed the veiled disapproval of his editor, and feared that his days of comfort and purpose might soon come to an end.

After a particularly violent confrontation with his superior (which arose from the exorbitant cost of an investigation into hotels east of Suez) Hilary made his way to Euston and bought a ticket to the farthest northern outpost of the LMS. He felt that a 'blind' journey like this was the only way to ease his humiliation and hoped that it would restore his lost wit and fluency with words.

As he settled himself into his First Class compartment at Euston he noticed one of the pictures above the seats. It showed an imposing hotel set against a background of sea and water. By some oversight

A First Class smokers' carriage

NWR porters at Euston, 1906

there was no caption to the painting. Hilary prided himself on his knowledge of the British railway system and felt annoyed when he found he could not identify the location. It nagged at him so greatly that on three occasions before the train started he got to his feet to re-examine the water-colour, certain that there must be some clue in the painting that he had overlooked. He racked his brains: sea and mountains spoke of Scotland, and the LNWR's old ties with the Caledonian made it quite possible that this was a Highland scene, yet he could not recall such a palatial establishment on the western seaboard of that country. There was a desert-island look to the place. The hotel appeared to be built on a spit of land projecting into the sea. Pine trees waved their branches above the dunes instead of palms, and in the distance a steamer puffed a plume of white vapour from its tall smokestack.

At the last moment before departure another passenger entered the compartment. He was tall and sallow and had old-fashioned side-whiskers. He nodded at Hilary without a smile, without speaking. As the express picked up speed beyond Watford, Hilary allowed his eyes to dwell again on the painting. His mind became occupied with an idle day-dream in which he was about to enter the hotel in the painting, but was prevented from doing so by a darkly dressed man who held his arm firmly at the elbow. But he knew that he must see inside the place and struggled to free himself. At last he did so but just as he mounted the steps to the entrance the sudden application of the brakes woke him with a heart-stopping shock. When he opened his eyes he saw the man in the corner seat watching him sardonically.

The train stood at Bletchley Station, where it was not scheduled to stop but had been checked by a signal. Hilary got to his feet, stretched, and looked once again at the painting. He knew at once that something in it had changed since he had last inspected it. The difference was not immediately apparent, but after a minute he recognised it. Two figures stood in front of the steps to the hotel: one had his arm on the other's elbow. The jolt he felt on seeing this was echoed by the train restarting. Through his shock, and through the roar of escaping steam from the labouring engine, Hilary heard his fellow passenger speak, though at first he was unable to distinguish the words, and had to ask him to repeat them.

'I said that the painting you are examining so closely is remarkable. It is unusual for a picture of such quality to enhance a railway compartment.'

'It was not so much the painting's quality which intrigued me', replied Hilary, 'but the subject. I thought I knew this country as well as anybody, but I am utterly perplexed as to where this building is situated. Are you able to put my mind at ease?'

'Indeed I am, sir.' As the stranger spoke the words he reached inside his valise to bring forth an ancient timetable. He shook out the map from its folds.

'If you look here you will see that the LNWR operated a steamer service across the Irish Sea to Greenore close by Carlingford. They had an interest in the Dundalk, Newry, and Greenore Railway who erected the hotel in the latter years of the last century. This timetable is many years out of date, but railways are a passion of mine, and I find it interesting to compare the working of lines today with that of twenty or so years ago, when the LMS had never been dreamt of.'

Hilary was never one to prolong a conversation needlessly, and on this occasion did little to maintain it, answering shortly to the comments and questions of his travelling-companion. Lulled by the rhythm of the rail-beats he soon fell asleep. When he awoke the express was drawing into Birmingham: the stranger had gone.

Left alone, Hilary felt a compulsion to study the painting yet again.

To his surprise the figures he had noticed earlier were no longer to be seen; neither was the steamboat in the picture. Furthermore there was a subtle change in the feeling of the painting. It was no longer a pleasing picture to behold, but seemed to have acquired a gloomy, sinister quality. The pine trees were swayed by the wind of an approaching squall which whipped up white horses from a sea that had previously been calm and inviting. No human figures were to be seen in the landscape which now seemed to speak only of dereliction and decay. Even as he studied the painting Hilary heard the sound of a shutter banging in the strengthening breeze; saw the flicker of a threadbare curtain as it blew outside a window whose glass had long been broken.

He shook his head, but it made no difference – the painting *was* changed. He opened the door: the bustle and noise of New Street Station appeared normal. He returned to his seat, his eyes fixed on the mysterious water-colour, but no further changes occurred. Nevertheless he now felt a new compulsion upon him and at Crewe took his farewell of the painting, alighted from the train and bought a ticket for Holyhead and the Irish mail-boat.

Ireland was one country that Hilary had neglected in his travels. There was good reason for this: its turmoil since the end of the war in 1918 had discouraged all but the most enthusiastic tourists, and only in the last year or so had things settled down so that visitors felt that they could explore the country in safety. However he felt little desire to sightsee. His intention was to get to Greenore as quickly as possible and set eyes on the mysterious hotel.

The journey came as a shock to his system. The mail-boat was crowded and since he had not made a reservation no cabins were available, in spite of his efforts to bribe the Purser. For once he neglected to put down his ill temper on paper, but instead drank whisky and water at the rowdy bar, feeling morose, frustrated and seasick.

His arrival in Dublin was hardly more auspicious. It happened that a great agricultural show was being held in the city; all the reputable hotels had been filled, and Hilary was forced to patronise a shabby boarding-house, full of theatre people, close to the station. It was the most squalid night he had spent in his life, the only consolation being the vitriolic comments on Ireland and its people he jotted down in his pocket-book.

Fortunately he was able to find a train to the north very early the next morning. Having paid for his accommodation the previous night he was able to escape from the house without having to suffer its breakfast. The journey to Dundalk took an hour and a half, and there he changed to the branch line to Greenore, the shabby six-wheeled carriages speaking for its decline in fortunes.

Within the hour he was at Greenore. The little train drew up at a large, covered-in terminus – much grander than the traffic would ever have seemed to warrant. As Hilary emerged from its portals into the fresh briny air he could see that its quays were still busy with ships. A venerable tramp-steamer was having its malodorous cargo of fertiliser unloaded, but of more interest was the object of the quest which stood almost opposite – the Greenore Hotel.

It now looked very different to how he had first seen it in the painting. The final version of the picture was very close to the truth. The optimism of its builders had been ill-founded even in the best of times. The outbreak of war in 1914, and the consequent abandonment of the steamer service between Holyhead and Greenore had been fatal. The railway managed to struggle on, though it carried few passengers. There was just enough freight and livestock traffic to allow it to survive, though its future was always problematical.

As he walked towards the hotel, Hilary felt a flash of *déjà vu* – an experience which he had only rarely encountered. In some previous existence he had been through these same actions, though he was

The Hotel at Greenore today

unable to remember the consequences: something deep within him warned that they would be unfortunate.

Lustreless green and cream paint peeled off the woodwork. The great doors were closed and locked. Many windows were broken and, as his premonition had warned, tattered lace curtains yellowed with grime blew outwards from some of those on the upper floors, propelled by a mysterious interior draught. He realised that his visit would be futile if he were to be unable to gain access to the place and so made his way back to the station, searching for a railway office which might, by chance, hold a key.

In this he was fortunate. By mentioning the names of several notables who served on the Board of the LMS (which he knew owned the branch line serving Greenore) he was able to persuade the Station Master that he was interested in purchasing the hotel and reviving the resort. By an oversight, he said, they had obviously forgotten to inform the local man-in-charge of his visit, but he hoped that there might be opportunities for mutual benefit in the future. Meanwhile, if he would care to receive a small token for his trouble . . .

Hilary only had rare occasions to use charm, and consequently it sounded graceless and insincere, but the man was won over by the proffered note, and handed over the keys of the hotel.

When he emerged he found that the weather had taken a sudden turn for the worse: rain was being driven horizontally by the wind to seek out every dry corner. Hilary drew up the collar of his light coat, but did not bother to use his umbrella, knowing that it would only be ruined by the fury of the wind. He hurried across to the stone stairway which led up to the main doorway of the hotel. Huddled close to the doors he unlocked them, and stepped inside.

As the Station Master had told him, an oil-lamp and matches had been left in the hall for those needing to explore the darkened rooms of the place. The hall was an imposing feature, meant to overpower the guest with its grandeur which reflected the benevolence and prosperity of the railway itself. As he crossed the marble floor his footsteps echoed up to the ceiling, so high that it was scarcely visible in the gloom. The sound disturbed many tiny residents of the deserted building, and their panic-stricken scurrying could be heard from all corners. The reception desk, covered by a thick layer of grey dust, was on the far side of the hall. The Visitors' Book lay open there: strangely the page at which it was opened was clear of dust, and almost of words too, except, and his heart sank as he read the

op: The terminus at Greenore, 1952

ottom: The 10.25 a.m. Dundalk to Greenore on Castletown Metal Bridge, 1954

The First Class Refreshment Room, Greenore Hotel

entry, for his own name and address, and the date of that very day.

Shaken and mystified he groped his way from the entrance hall to another room. By chance it was the dining-room, with several tables and chairs left in their original positions. With relief Hilary sat down, placing his lamp on the table before him. For some time his mind was occupied puzzling over the events that had befallen him since he had embarked on the train at Euston. No natural explanation could suffice for the changes which had happened to the picture, or for the way his name had come to be in the Visitors' Book. As his eyes became accustomed to the dimness of the light, Hilary also became aware of the unwelcome feeling that he was not alone in the room. He glanced around. Mirrors reflected the room from the far wall, though they were so begrimed that the dark outlines of the furniture were blurred. But one feature was distinct: the silhouette of the figure in front of the reflected daylight of the only unshuttered window. Yet how could that be? – for if the reflection was real, then the person would be sitting opposite him at his table: yet assuredly no one was there. But that is where the voice came from, and there was a moment before he recognised it: then he placed it – it was the voice of the man on the train, the man in the corner seat.

'They will be lean years for you, my friend, if you carry on. There will be no further pleasures in this existence.'

The image in the mirror was lucid now – Hilary saw again the sardonic features of his travelling companion of the day before, who continued:

'You can draw your conclusions about who I may be. My talents are many but I take particular delight in devising amusing retributions for those who have wrought suffering on others. I cannot claim to be of this earth or of the other unworldly places, yet I have the power to inflict the direst discomforts on those whom I choose to attend. You may be interested to hear what lies ahead in your life should you choose to survive your visit to this place.

'When, or if, you return to your office you will find a new face at your desk. The proprietor of your journal has a niece, a bright young thing who has always had a wish to travel. Unfortunately she is not able to express herself on paper adequately and so you will become her amanuensis, her "ghost", I believe the expression is, if you will pardon the term. Your salary will be severely reduced, of course, and you will lose all the luxuries and privileges you have enjoyed hitherto.

'My knowledge of your character suggests to me that you will reject this offer, and your anger expressed to your employer will ensure that no other suitable post will be open to you in Fleet Street. In time you will become a penniless recluse, a repulsive specimen who will, in the end, take to drink and be forced on the streets. A soup kitchen will provide an unfortunate cuisine for one who has fed so richly in the past. I believe that the fate I have reserved for you in some measure equates the viciousness and cruelty you have extended to others by the acid of your pen. Many have been thrown on to the streets because of your comments in the past. Now it is your turn.'

With a movement of fine elegance the stranger's reflection nodded to itself and silence descended on the dusty room. After a long pause Hilary's shaking voice uttered his question:

'And, sir, what course can I take to avoid this fate? Am I allowed to turn a new leaf? I can see my faults, sir, my arrogance and hurtfulness, and I can truly promise that I will not fail in becoming good.'

Another pause followed, as though these remarks were being considered, and then came the reply:

'I am afraid not. But I will allow you an alternative. Indeed, as I am not without compassion, and as this location is so eminently suitable, I think I will ordain it a compulsion. Come with me, Mr Gore.'

As these words were uttered, the figure of the stranger stepped from the mirror and headed for the door of the dining-room. There seemed to be no necessity now for a lamp, and Hilary left it at the table as he followed his strange companion who noiselessly glided through the hall and began to ascend the stairs.

Their way led to the very top of the building, through dusty corridors, up crumbling back stairways. At last they arrived at a low, narrow doorway in one of the attic rooms.

'Your path lies through there. Make haste, or time will run out for you.'

With these words said, the stranger disappeared, melted into his surroundings. After a moment of amazement at this, Hilary obediently opened the door and climbed over a step on to the roof. Rain lashed his face, the wind tugged at his clothes. He moved to the low parapet. His mind was saying: 'It looks good on the grass down there. Look, you could jump to the beach from here! Fly like a seagull – just step off the parapet . . .'

As he leapt Hilary expected to wake from a falling nightmare, but he never did. His spreadeagled body was found by the Station Master an hour or so later, and there was a great deal of speculation at the misdeeds a man like that must have perpetrated to give his soul to everlasting torment in such a way.

Meanwhile, back at the offices of *The Graphic* in Fleet Street, a smiling, attractive young girl sat down at Hilary Gore's desk and began leafing through Bradshaw.

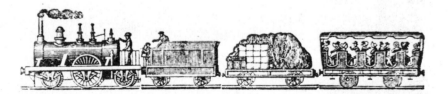

Judgement Day

The wires below rattled and the semaphore at the end of the platform dropped. Once again the Norwich train would be at least thirty minutes late. I had spent the time recalling to my mind the changes that had befallen the railway in my lifetime. I could remember when this small market town was a busy junction with two branch lines. Even as late as the 1960s there were two waiting-rooms here, one of which would have had a coal fire should the weather warrant it, as well as the ever-welcoming station buffet. This was presided over by the aptly named Dolly who, though she must have weighed about seventeen stone, possessed the features and colouring of a china doll. Instead of being cold and miserable waiting for a delayed pay-train one would have been warmed by a blazing fire and by the company of Dolly and those who gathered round her. She had been in charge of the buffet-bar for the best part of twenty years and was the catalyst who opened up the personalities of her customers. A good story was always to be found there, and one would trigger another, aided by the aura of well-being stimulated by the appreciative company and the excellent ale.

Many of the stories gained in the telling each time they were narrated, but one I can vouch for as I was present when the events

A typical LNER village station – Middleton Towers

began, and saw the way in which they affected the man concerned.

Ted Griffiths was also known as Ted the Boot since he was Welsh and a commercial traveller who sold leather and other bits and pieces to the shoe trade. He was a salesman of the old school and preferred to travel by train for the simple reason that you could always depend on finding someone to chat with. Ted was a very sociable being: you felt warmed by his presence and, unusually for a good story-teller, he was an attentive listener as well. I was in the station buffet on the day that he was asked to judge the Tidy Station Competition.

As he said afterwards, he only did it for a bit of a laugh, to help out his old friend Hugh Summers, the District Superintendent. Hugh had been let down at the last moment by a local worthy who had promised to do the job. The competition was designed to stimulate rural Station Masters into keeping their stations presentable. Before Nationalisation the judge would have been a Director, who would have been taken down the line in the Directors' Saloon, and lavishly wined and dined at the Company's expense. However the State now owned the railways and with their austerity measures the pattern had been changed. Instead of the luxury of the Directors' Saloon a wooden bench was rigged across the front buffers of a venerable tender locomotive. It was chilly, and somewhat hard on the bottom, but was an excellent way of enjoying the scenery. It was arranged that Ted should be at the station first thing on the following Saturday and would be transported to the line that he was to judge.

He found his engine panting gently at a bay platform, the bench bolted securely in place (he inspected it closely). A guard had been detailed to travel with him, but he made it plain that he preferred the comfort of the cab, and the company of the crew, to the bench in front.

'You'll soon get used to it,' he reassured Ted as he tucked a large travelling-rug about him, 'it's quite safe.'

Nevertheless at first Ted felt exposed and foolish, especially when they passed through level-crossings where the waiting people pointed and laughed. However as the journey progressed he began to enjoy himself. The village Station Masters and their wives proved to be pleasant and welcoming. There were trays of coffee and home-baked cakes, as well as the odd dram or two, as the Station Masters explained their difficulties in raising a really good floral display, what with the blight on the marigolds, etc.

Lunch was taken at an inn adjoining the largest station on the line – the crossing-point of two rural railways. Here Ted found the company of the driver, fireman, and guard particularly convivial, and all four were in a benign frame of mind when they left the place shortly after closing-time.

'Only two more stations,' said the driver, climbing back on to the footplate, 'the others don't count.'

It was a fair run to the next station, and the weather, which earlier had seemed calm and set fair, now hinted at a change as storm clouds grew above the pleasantly rolling Suffolk countryside. Ted dozed off, his senses lulled by the rhythm of the wheels and by the liquor he had consumed at lunchtime (he had restricted himself to spirits as beer would have been inconvenient in the circumstances). He awoke as the engine shuddered to a halt at a pleasant station.

'Ah! this is the winner,' Ted thought as he took in the whitewashed flints which surrounded the colourful, weedless, flower-beds. The display was at its best – aubretia, pansies, primulas, and a multitude of fragrant lilac trees. Even the station buildings looked scrubbed and freshly painted. It was a winner even before a buxom, smiling lady (the Station Master's wife, naturally) appeared, bearing a tray with hot scones and strong tea.

The next station, however, was almost as good. Obviously there was a rivalry between the two places. Here he was offered more tea, this time accompanied by sandwiches with gentleman's relish, and a

Soham Station, pre-war

dark and rich fruit cake. The Station Master was an amiable old boy, due to retire in a couple of years, who had won the previous two competitions. He had served in the same regiment as Ted, and they reminisced about mutual friends and enemies. They ended by drinking each other's health with generous tots of a rare Scotch, and then Ted climbed hazily back on to his perch and settled himself comfortably for the final part of the journey.

Once again he was soothed by the regular beat of wheels on rails. He was on the edge of sleep when he was disturbed by a change of rhythm as the engine slowed and then clattered over a couple of sets of points. He opened his eyes. The threat of rain seemed about to become a reality. The sky was almost as dark as night and there was a heaviness about the air which felt somehow unnatural.

The train drew up at the deserted platform, but Ted felt no inclination to move for a moment as he took in the lifeless scene. The station seemed normal enough – there were milk-churns and a few

parcels waiting for the arrival of a train – yet there was no one there to greet the engine and its important passenger, which to Ted's mind was surprising in view of his welcome at previous stations.

He got down from his seat on to the platform. His limbs were stiff and he was surprised by the strange chill wind that suddenly struck his face. He glanced about. The dim branches of the trees were motionless, and the steam and smoke from the engine rose straight to the dark sky. There was no sign of the crew; Ted assumed they must be taking the opportunity to brew up, and so set out along the platform to explore the station.

He noticed with disapproval that the few flower-beds were overgrown with weeds. Similarly the topiary had been left to itself for too long and was now untidy and shapeless. Remarkably the waiting-room windows still wore their crosses of gummed paper put up in wartime to prevent the glass splintering and flying. The posters were old too, warning of the dangers of gossiping in the presence of

The aftermath at Soham (and two previous illustrations)

strangers ('Look out! There's a spy about!'). Ted felt he was back in a vanished world. He picked up a discarded newspaper. The headline said:

BATTLE FOR ROME BEGINS
German Line Pierced on Anzio Front

Hardly feeling surprise at this he looked for the date – 1 June 1944. He shook his head, but the image remained unaltered. Still feeling dazed at the implications he left the waiting-room and returned to the platform. Where was he? He looked at the seats, but the nameplates had been carefully removed from each one – another wartime security measure, designed to confuse an invader, which proved far more troublesome to Britons fighting in obscure corners of the realm. However the signal-box stood on the platform, and he knew that he was certain to find the identity of the place there. Although no one was on duty (and in the circumstances he had hardly expected to find anyone there) he was easily able to discover the place. The line diagram and telegraph told him that he was at Soham, on the edge of the Fens. This was logical, he reflected, since the previous station had been Fordham. Then it came on him. Soham Station had been blown up in the latter part of the war, and had only been rebuilt to a very basic, functional pattern, without the usual station house, goods office, or other trimmings. In fact the modern station was little more than a glorified halt. Yet the station before him now was completely Victorian. This, then, was a nightmare. He pinched himself, hard. The deserted signal-box and its surroundings remained real. Could this be worse than a nightmare then? Ted looked round at the furnishings of the box – the train register book was open on the desk. Just four entries had been made on the page. Without looking to see what they were he tore out the page and put it in his pocket. Then he left the box, descending the few steps to the platform, and returned to the locomotive. He wanted no more of the place, and feared meeting people who might belong there. He settled himself on the bench and drew his rug about him. Closing his eyes, he felt the engine begin to move as he drifted into a deep sleep.

They had to shake him to bring him to his senses at Ely. The events of the latter part of his journey came back to him immediately. He felt in his pocket – the piece of paper was still there!

'Enjoy your trip then, guv'nor?'

The engine-driver had come round to say farewell.

'Yes, thanks, it's been an interesting day. I'll look for you now, when I use the train. Have one on me, you and your mate, when you clock off.'

He gave the driver a ten shilling note and boarded the train for Norwich which waited at the through platform opposite. Seated in the compartment he examined the precious scrap of paper. It was dated 2 June 1944, and the last entry read: '12.15 a.m. ex-March Whitemoor. 51 wagons, Earls Colne. Accepted 3.07 a.m.'

There were no difficulties about discovering the events of that horrific night at Soham, though the newspapers of the time were wary of disclosing the identity of the place concerned. Accounts of the disaster came from 'a Cambridgeshire town' though later it was admitted that this was Soham. Both the driver of the train, Gimbert, and his fireman, Nightfall, were awarded the George Cross for their bravery. Unhappily the honour was given to the young fireman posthumously. It was he who left the footplate to uncouple the train when they noticed that the leading van was on fire. There were forty 500-pound bombs on this wagon, and each of the other vans were loaded with similar amounts of high explosives. The train had reached the northern outskirts of Soham at this time, so they planned to uncouple the van from the remainder of the train and run it through the station to a cutting which would shelter the town from the full force of the explosion (cuttings are a rarity in the Fens). Nightfall managed to knock the couplings apart with a heavy hammer, and climbed back into the cab of the massive WD 2–8–0 locomotive. They carried on to Soham, slowing at the station so that they could warn the signalman of the train standing to the north of the station. Seeing something was wrong, the signalman had left his box and was waiting for them on the platform. As the driver leaned towards him to tell him of their predicament the wagon exploded. The fireman was killed outright: the signalman died soon after in hospital. Driver Gimbert, a man of eighteen stone, was hurled over two hundred yards by the explosion but survived, although badly injured. The crater underneath the wagon was fifteen feet deep and sixty-six feet across. Although virtually every window in Soham was broken by the explosion, and some seven hundred houses damaged, the heroism of the fireman and driver in uncoupling the train saved the town from complete devastation. How easy it would have been for them to have abandoned the train and run to shelter.

All of Ted's drinking companions noticed the change in him after his jaunt. Slowly he recovered his former high spirits, though a year passed before he told them the story. Much later he confessed to visiting Soham each year on 2 June to see whether the ghost station would reappear, and thus confirm the evidence of the soiled and crumpled scrap of paper which he would produce with a triumphant flourish as he concluded his account of the adventure.

The Happy Children

The train rattled across the lonely countryside. It was dusk on a damp, still November afternoon. There were few passengers in its two carriages, and only empty milk-churns in the van at the front. In the last compartment at the rear of the train a small boy sat with his mother, his face buried in her coat.

'But a house can't hurt *you*,' she said, 'specially one you only see once in a blue moon. You're a big boy now, to be frightened by such nonsense.'

There was no response to this, so she twisted a lock of curly brown hair between her fingers, and looked again out of the window at the darkening landscape. There were no pinpoints of light to be seen anywhere: it was wartime and the black-out was rigorously enforced, even in this remote district.

The train began to slow down, swerved over some points, across a

A 'Super Claud' (Class D16/3) deep in the Norfolk countryside near Burnham Market

level-crossing and then the sound of its wheels became loud suddenly as a dark shape loomed out of the darkness and then was gone.

'There,' she said, 'we've passed your silly old house. You can look up now; we'll be at Fransham in a moment.'

Cautiously the boy raised his head from her lap and peered out of the window. With brakes squealing the train drew up at a deserted platform, and the boy and his mother began collecting up their belongings. The woman fumbled for a moment with the leather window-strap before she was able to open the door, then got down with the ancient, swollen suitcase. With easy, practised grace she lifted the boy from the carriage and slammed the door shut. The engine whistled, and then jerkily began to pull away from the station.

'Goodness, I hope Uncle's here to meet us,' she said, taking her son's hand and lifting the suitcase. 'I wouldn't fancy walking to the farm in the dark.'

But she need not have feared. Outside the booking-hall the old trap waited. Uncle Alfred was by the horse's head, deep in conversation with an American airman. His weathered, wrinkled face lit up with pleasure as he saw them.

'Well, bless my old boots, if that ain't the gal now with the young'un. By rights I should have seen you off the train and lugged that there case of yours, but this gentleman has been telling me how he stacks peas in the States and I quite lost track of time. Come on, give us that case here.'

The woman and the boy were soon seated in the trap, the latter clutching a small packet of chewing-gum that the American had given him. 'We'll see you at the house, then,' Uncle shouted, as the airman climbed into his jeep. He jerked at the reins to start the horse on their short journey home.

The lane was narrow with steep banks and crossed the railway by the black house that frightened the boy. It was almost completely dark now: even so he still turned his head away as they passed it. His uncle noticed this:

'You're a rum 'un, young Will, letting that old cottage bother you! Why it's only held up by the tar it's daubed with.'

This was true: the black pitch kept the weather out and held the decaying clay lump together. Even so an end wall had to be propped up. It all went to make up an evil, threatening picture in the boy's mind. From his earliest childhood he had associated it with witches, ghosts and hobgoblins. Even now, at the great age of six, he was

unwilling to abandon these terrors lightly: the horror had a pleasurable fascination about it.

At last they reached New Farm. They rattled up the track which crossed the front meadow and came to a halt by the back door, which was immediately opened. Aunt Ada stood at the threshold, her massive frame silhouetted by the dim light of oil-lamps beyond. Her welcome was typically warm and effusive:

'You must both be perished being in that there trap without a rug. I told Alfred to get them out for you, but no, he wouldn't have it, and now you're blue with the cold. Come on in and get warm by the oven.'

There was a vast range at the end of the kitchen with comfortable old chairs drawn up around it. Aunt Ada threw open the doors of the oven and the front of the grate so that the glow soon warmed their faces and their outstretched hands. Cups of tea with bread and scones toasted on the range followed, and Will and his mother were made to feel that this was their true home, not their 'little old rabbit-hutch' (Alfred's words) in the city.

The following couple of hours or so were taken up in catching up on family gossip – then the talk was of the village.

'There's new people in the Crossing House now, a foreign lady and her daughter. That's the house your Will don't like. The girl must be about his age. It might be that she'd like his company. There's not many youngsters this end of the village.'

Later that week pressure was brought to bear on Will to pay a visit to the black house so that he might get to know the young girl. All efforts having failed in this, a compromise was agreed: the girl was invited to tea.

She came on the Saturday of the same week. She was pretty, with blue eyes and fair hair, and although shy at first she was unable to restrain her natural vivacity for long. The children were friends by the end of the afternoon. It did not seem to matter in the slightest that neither could understand a word the other said: Olde was a Norwegian refugee and had yet to learn English.

The long winter holiday turned out to be heaven for both children. The restraints laid on them by the war could be forgotten in the country, and they dashed about over farm and fields, their shouts and screams drowning even the noise of the American bombers taking off from the airfield close by. Will even overcame his terror of the black house, and was taken home by Olde to meet her mother who at least spoke English. At Christmas the children gave each other presents – a knitted doll for Olde, a beautiful wooden lorry for Will – but soon afterwards he had to make a tearful farewell and return with his mother to the city, and to school.

It seemed ages before Easter came and Will and his mother could return to New Farm. They left the city early on a crisp morning, the brilliant sunshine making even the bomb-shattered buildings look beautiful. A train crowded with airmen and soldiers took them to King's Lynn, where they changed to the dawdling little train (hauled by an engine built sixty years before) which would take them to Fransham.

This time the boy was eager to see the black house. He leant from the window, braving the cold wind and smuts from the engine, desperately trying to catch an early glimpse of it. Then he could see the white crossing-gates and its dark outline just beyond: but something had changed – the thatched roof had gone, charred rafters pointed to the sky, an end wall had fallen. Sensing disaster, Will threw himself into his mother's arms, and he was still sobbing inconsolably when the train drew up at the station.

Uncle Alfred was waiting on the platform, his face not wearing its usual happy smile. He guessed the reason for the boy's grief at once and said quietly: 'It were a right terrible thing that happened the other night. They reckon it was a chimney fire that started it. Once that got a hold the thatch took fire, and both of them asleep in their beds. But they say as how it were the smoke killed them and not the flames, so they could never have suffered or anything.'

Will was sick with grief. He spent three days in bed, crying for long hours at a time. When he finally seemed to have recovered his relatives were careful to keep him away from the scene of the tragedy, but at the end of the week he was able to escape their attention and took himself off to the burnt-down house.

An observer, during the next few days, seeing the boy alone, might have had worries about his sanity. He wandered about his old happy haunts which he had shared with Olde, speaking in a clear, normal voice. His mother, anxious when she was unable to find him about the farm, at last tracked him down and spent some time listening. She soon discovered that he was not truly talking to himself: his words were addressed to his dead friend. He was busy explaining to her the things he had learnt at school, telling her of the new friends he had made, of the fresh games that they could now play together. Alarmed by this his mother broke the spell by taking him in her arms and hugging him, reproaching him for going off on his own leaving her to worry. Then she asked him who he had been speaking to.

'Why Olde, of course. She's very happy in Heaven but a bit lonely and wants to know what I'm doing. It's good that I can talk to her now and she understands what I say.'

The next day the boy left the farmhouse early and failed to return at lunchtime. His mother, uncle, aunt and the cowman spent much of the afternoon searching for him, but without success. He turned up for tea quite unconcerned. Angrily he was told he had no business to go off on his own for so long.

'But I had to look for Olde's dolly. She left him in the woods and told me where I could find him and I did. She was worried about him getting cold and wet.' Sure enough he was clutching the woollen doll, soggy and somewhat soiled.

'Tomorrow she wants me to see if the thrush's eggs have hatched out. She's told me where the nest is, but I might be a bit late.'

Listening on the stairs that night his mother heard his sleepy voice

73

retelling Olde the bedtime story he had just been read. When she explained her concern to Aunt Ada the old lady shrugged her shoulders and said not to worry – 'He'll get over it.'

But Will's involvement with the dead girl continued to grow in intensity during the remaining days of his stay at the farm. He had to pay daily visits to the thrush's nest to make sure that the fledglings were thriving. He was told to wave at a particular engine-driver every time he passed because he had been Olde's friend and was sure to be missing her, and he had to seek out Larry O'Brien, an American airman who spoke Norwegian, to tell him that Olde was safe and happy in Heaven.

At last it was time to go home. Will wept many tears the night before and did his best to persuade his mother to postpone their departure, but to no avail: they left on the midday train.

Back at home in the city Will was sullen and lacklustre. His teacher commented on his lack of enthusiasm, and his mother had to explain to her the tragic circumstances of his holiday and its subsequent effects. At night, after prayers, Will could again be heard talking to his dead friend. He would turn over the pages in his picture-books, describing to her the illustrations which he found particularly pleasing. Each evening his mother listened at the door of his room until the small voice grew slow with sleep and finally drifted into silence.

Gradually, over about a month, things began to return to normal. Will seemed less obsessed by the little girl and his mother ceased to listen for his bedtime conversations until late one night she heard the sound of passionate weeping coming from his bedroom. She comforted him as best as she was able and asked him why he was so upset.

'It's because Olde thinks I don't love her any more. She wants me to go and see the Crossing House again: she thinks someone's going to live there again and doesn't want them to. Will you come with me?'

His mother gently explained how impossible that would be for them now. He had his school and she had a wartime job making radios for aeroplanes; she would get into terrible trouble if she went gallivanting without good reason.

At last he turned his head to the wall and seemed quiet and about to sleep. As she left the room he said: 'It would be awful if she was angry with me, wouldn't it?'

The following afternoon Will's mother got home at her usual time and went to the neighbour's house to collect her son. He should have been there but was not. They had assumed that he must have had to do some errand for her, and had afterwards gone straight home. Frantic with worry she called on Will's schoolfriends to see if, by any chance, he had lingered with them on the way home, but no, none had seen him after school. In desperation she visited the Headmaster and Will's teacher, but they too were unable to shed light on his disappearance. She went with them to the police.

A full-scale search was launched the next morning. Volunteers marched across the commons and allotments, looked into sheds and garages, and pulled rakes through ponds. At the end of the day one of the searchers, a policeman, looked at her sadly:

'I think we've done just about all we can here. Is there anywhere he might have gone – to relatives or friends away from the city?'

Immediately his mother thought of the farm, and of the little boy's grief two nights before.

'It's just possible he might have gone to his uncle's farm in Norfolk. But if he had they would have let me know, unless he's not got there yet.'

'Well, it's worth a phone call,' replied the policeman. 'Now what's the name of his uncle?'

In fact his mother was right in thinking that Will had gone to Fransham. It was easy to pretend to be a train-spotter, to buy a platform ticket and board the train to King's Lynn (he spent the journey in the toilet); easier still to get on the branch-line train without paying. It was dark when he arrived at his destination. He slipped quietly from the train and hid in the shadows until it drew away from the station. Then he made his way back down the line towards the Crossing House. He spent the night in a lineside hut only a little distance from the ruin, talking to Olde, reassuring her that they would soon be as happy as they had ever been.

At dawn he stood by the ruins of the black house, waiting. He was not to be disappointed – as the sun rose, so a figure in white joyfully ran down the path towards him.

'Let's play, let's play,' he shouted, and hand in hand they ran to all the places they had loved before, exploring them again and finding fresh delights.

Talking later of that day many of the villagers spoke of half-seeing a young girl and boy racing about the woods and fields. No one was ever close enough to have a good look at them, but all spoke of the feeling of pure happiness that seemed to flood through them on seeing the children at play.

The last train from Lynn was never a very busy one on that line – it dawdled its way across the countryside bearing just a dozen or so servicemen back to their bases. At the inquest, most attention was paid to the evidence of its engine-driver:

'It were just about dark when I came up to the crossing at Fransham. We weren't going too quick on account of slowing for the station. As we got to the gates I saw two children a-chasing each other. There was a young girl in white. She came to the side gate and I thought "she's left it wholly late to cross". But she opened the gate and dashed across with just enough to spare; but the boy followed, and we caught him. We was going so slow he must have seen us, but he ran right across under the wheels, I never had a chance to touch the brake. . . .'

Over the years, until the passing of the railway, there were many accounts of 'the happy children'. As time went by their appearances became less frequent and less distinct. The unwritten, unspoken taboo of the village, which discouraged anyone from rebuilding on the site of the Crossing House, was at last forgotten and strangers to the district erected a charmless red-brick residence on the site. However they were not there for long. The little boy of the house began to speak of the marvellous games he was having with two children, a boy and a girl, who were always so happy. . . .

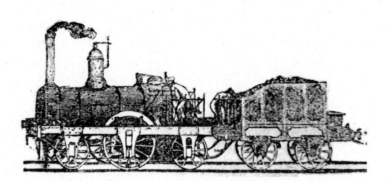

Turning the Table

Snotter was always the cheekiest of us engine-spotters, and the first to get into any mischief that was going. He once got me locked into an empty luggage-van and I was dead lucky not to end up at Hunstanton. Another time he pushed my brother Eric into the pond which fed the water-tower, and after that we weren't allowed out to go spotting for all of a month.

We certainly knew our way about, in those days. Although the loco staff turned a pretty tolerant eye on us, we had to be a bit crafty with the Station Master and the inspectors. We hated buying platform tickets, mainly because we rarely had a penny spare to pay for them, and so had to sneak on to the station to get to the best vantage points. From the end of Platform 2 we could see right down to the sheds, and it was also good for spotting the through trains. Furthermore it was so far from the station buildings that the inspectors seldom bothered to chase us off once we had reached it. There we stood, in all weathers, our notebooks and Spotters' Guides at the ready, waiting for a 'cop', a rare visitor to our shed, perhaps of a class we had never seen before.

Many of the engine crews befriended us, sometimes allowing us up

The Great Eastern terminus at Hunstanton, now a car park

on the footplate for a moment or two. If we went down to the shed they might be persuaded to show us round, though more often we got seen off by the Locomotive Superintendent and his staff. Looking back you can see his point, for it was a dark and dangerous place for young boys to be let loose in, and accidents were fairly frequent there, even among enginemen who were supposed to know their way about.

To Snotter the Spotter, of course, to be banned from a place was a challenge. He was always hovering on the approaches to the sheds plotting ways to get in, but ready to flee from the wrath of the staff who were, by now, heartily sick of his cheek and mischief.

It was many years later that I learned the full story of poor Snotter's downfall, from an old engine-driver who was a permanent fixture in my local pub. Apparently the younger members of the staff at the shed decided to teach Snotter a lesson. They lured him into the yard, caught him, soaked him with water from a hose on one of the loco's tenders, and then rolled him in the ash-pit. He got into terrible trouble from his parents for this, and wasn't allowed out for ages. He swore vengeance against those who had treated him in such a rough and treacherous manner. Snotter could be vicious against his enemies.

Small things began to go wrong at the shed. Fire-irons disappeared, to be found many months later in the most unlikely of places. One set of irons so successfully jammed the turntable that it was out of action

for two days. Fog-detonators let off immediately outside the convenience when someone was in residence did not improve the peace of mind of the staff either. Snotter crept around the shed doing as much mischief as he could. Occasionally he was seen, and was once hit by a large lump of coal thrown from a footplate, but he took care not to be caught again. Spurred on by these successes his pranks became more spectacular, and dangerous.

He discovered how to put an engine in gear, and how to keep its regulator open. Cleaners would light the fire in the firebox of a 'cold' engine, and then it would be left for a time to look after itself. If a gremlin happened to meddle with the controls at this time, the results could be catastrophic. On two occasions engines moved off into the yard of their own accord, as their fires burned up and the steam pressure increased to a working level. In the first incident the engine crashed into a number of empty coal-wagons by the coaling-stage, doing a considerable amount of damage. The second time the loco would have run on to the main line had catch-points not derailed it first. After this the police were alerted, and though there was nothing to prove that Snotter had a hand in the accidents, his parents were told of the dire consequences that could come of his meddling and so kept a very tight rein on him indeed.

Whether Snotter did, in fact, have anything to do with the third accident will never be known. About six months after the derailment of the runaway engine, another runaway caused the death of our favourite driver, Sam Larkins. Sam had his B17, *Raby Castle*, over the inspection-pit at the time, and had climbed up among the gears to do the oiling. A 'Super Claud' suddenly began to roll down the same track and hit the B17. Poor old Sam was so caught up with his loco's innards that it took the fire brigade two hours to cut him out, by which time he was dead. Again, nothing could be proved against Snotter, but neither did anyone believe that he had *not* done it, and in the end his parents moved away from the place.

There the story could have ended, had the railway not been so strongly in Snotter's blood. When he left school, three years later, he applied for a job as an apprentice engine-cleaner in the town where the family then lived. This place was also served by the LNER but was far enough away for his exploits not to be known there. Years passed – the railways were Nationalised, and Snotter became a fireman, at first confined to shunting duties about his home yard, but eventually he was promoted and became a fireman on the main line.

Derby Loco Shed No. 4 (by gaslight) 1910

The day previous to his death, Snotter had worked a special from his home shed in the north to the town of his birth. The return working was to be the next day, a Sunday, and after sleeping at the hostel he had risen early to tend his engine in the shed. He didn't trust the local cleaners to raise steam as he knew them to be unfamiliar with his class of loco. In any case, the shift did not begin until 4.30 a.m., and Snotter knew an earlier start had to be made if the engine was to be ready to leave with its train at 6.45.

So the shed was deserted when he got there, its atmosphere as murky as he remembered, the uncanny noises of water gurgling and metal contracting startling him from time to time as boilers and fireboxes cooled down. Carefully Snotter built his fire. Soon there was pressure enough in the boiler to take the locomotive on to the turntable for turning. This was a delicate job that a fireman always enjoyed, for the centre of balance had to be exact to within half an inch if the table was to turn easily, loaded with more than 160 tons of loco. At last Snotter was satisfied that he had his beast exactly right and screwed down the brake. He climbed from the cab and made his way to the push-bar, knowing that it was going to be a struggle to turn it single-handed (the motor that used to turn it using the loco's own steam pressure had long been out of order). By using all his strength he managed to get the thing moving; then it was easy and he began to get concerned about how he was going to stop it at the right set of tracks without damaging the ratchet. Accordingly, he dodged to the other side of the push-bar, put his back against it and dug in his heels to slow the great weight down. As he did so he saw with horror the engine on his left begin to move forward. He had three seconds to see that it was going to be in his path and used half of this time desperately putting more of his strength against the unstoppable weight pushing him forward. In his last moments he had time to realise that there was no escaping an awful death, which at least had the merit of being swift and distinctive. The bar broke his back before slamming into the side of the runaway and breaking off. The turntable continued to revolve for many minutes unattended, and was still moving slowly when the cleaners arrived some minutes later.

The official inquiry could find no explanation for the movement of the loco which fouled the turntable. Its fire was unlit, and it was sworn that the wheels had been chocked. Only the older hands at the shed thought of an answer to the mystery, when they found out the unfortunate victim had been Snotter.

Irish Jack

I was a long time looking, in that remote, lonely churchyard, but at last I found it. Lichen made the inscription difficult to decipher, but the upper letters were clear enough:

'John Gibbon, known as Irish Jack, navigator and musician, found dead in a snowstorm at Flordon, January 3rd, 1844.'

After this the letters were harder to read, being more weathered and screened by vegetation, but eventually the remainder of the words were revealed:

'This stone was raised from subscriptions offered by his workmates: "The memory of the just is blessed: but the name of the wicked shall rot." Proverbs X.'

This was the first clue in my quest to solve a mystery that had become very personal to me. I had seen a ghost, not once but on many occasions, and had become strangely fond of him, though I was not to know then of the frightful end to the haunting which I shall relate. At least I now felt sure that I knew the identity of the spectre.

My haunting had begun on a January night, very many years ago now; in fact so long ago that only steam locomotives used the main line, and those ran in the liveries of the pre-Nationalised companies. I worked a lonely signal-box in south Norfolk, on the Great Eastern line between Norwich and Ipswich, and that night I was on late shift. It was a walk of some three miles from my cottage to the box, a fair way of it along the track. It was a wild night, the wind buffeting at my face, bearing half-hearted flurries of snow which hinted at heavier falls later. I was carrying an oil-lantern which for a time gave out a meagre, flickering light, until a particularly boisterous squall blew out the flame. This did not trouble me unduly as I knew my path well, and once by the tracks could hardly lose my way.

When I first heard the sound I thought it was a trick of the wind, in branches and telegraph wires, perhaps. But I soon realised that I was not mistaken and I was truly hearing the sound of the bag-pipes. Their music is always evocative of wide, lonely spaces, and there is a sadness in it which seems to come from the depths of the soul. I knew instinctively that the lament which was being played came from no earthly source, but I was intrigued rather than frightened. The sorrowful sound came to an end after a minute or so, and then I distinctly heard the wheezy noise

SACRED

TO THE MEMORY OF THOMAS SCAIFE,

late an Engineer on the Birmingham and Gloucester Railway, who lost his life at Bromsgrove Station, by the Explosion of an Engine Boiler, on Tuesday the 10 of November 1840.

He was 28 Years of Age, highly esteemed by his fellow workmen for his many amiable qualities, and his Death will be long lamented by all those who had the pleasure of his acquaintance.

The following lines were composed by an unknown Friend as a Memento of the worthiness of the Deceased.

My engine now is cold and still,   My flanges all refuse to guide,
No water does my boiler fill: My clacks, also, though once so strong,
My coke affords its flame no more,   Refuse to aid the busy throng,
My days of usefulness are o'er,   No more I feel each urging breath,
My wheels deny their noted speed   My steam is now condens'd in death.
No more my guiding hands they heed   Life's railway's o'er, each station's past,
My whistle too, has lost its tone,   In death I'm stopp'd and rest at last.
Its shrill and thrilling sounds are gone. Farewell dear friends and cease to weep,
My valves are now thrown open wide, In Christ I'm safe, in Him I sleep.

THIS STONE WAS ERECTED AT THE JOINT EXPENCE
OF HIS FELLOW WORKMEN 1842

PRATT, Eng.

SACRED

TO THE MEMORY OF JOSEPH RUTHERFORD,

LATE ENGINEER TO THE BIRMINGHAM AND GLOUCESTER RAILWAY COMPANY

who Died Nov 11 1840 Aged 32 Years

Oh! Reader stay, and cast an eye,
Upon this Grave wherein I lie,
For cruel Death has challenged me,
And soon alas! will call on thee;
Repent in time, make no delay,
For Christ will call you all away.

My time was spent like dew in sun,
Beyond all cure, my glass is run.

THIS STONE WAS ERECTED BY HIS AFFECTIONATE
RELICT 1841

that pipes make when the air is expelled at the finish of a piece.

Several times during the course of that winter (a particularly hard, long one) I thought I caught further snatches of the lament, but they were fainter than on the first occasion, and I could never be certain that I was not deluding myself. However the events of the following winter completely convinced me of the existence of the ghost and provided me with a few clues as to his identity.

It was a brilliant moonlit night, again in midwinter, when I had my first visual encounter with Irish Jack. I clearly heard the sound of the pipes just after the up mail had passed. This time I was on the steps of the box, having just taken the coal-scuttle down for replenishment, when I heard the unearthly music. I glanced down the track, and within a stone's throw could see a figure which I knew must be the phantom piper. The moonlight gave his outline a faintly luminous quality and also removed all vestige of colour from the figure (though I suspected that there was little there anyway). However it did allow me to take in the details of his dress and appearance. The strongest impression that I gained of him was his aura of sadness, which was emphasised by the music he played. For some curious reason I was unable to see the expression on his features, but I knew from his stance that it would be sorrowful. I could see there was something unusual about the way he played the pipes: rather than blow into the

bag in the style of the Scots, he used bellows worked by the movement of an elbow against his side to inflate them (I subsequently learned that this is the way that the Irish play their bagpipes). His dress was shabby and utterly unlike anything I had come across before: stained baggy trousers made of a canvas-like material, a nondescript waistcoat which showed a multitude of seams (later research revealed that the navvies of yesteryear were particularly fond of moleskin waistcoats), and a length of homespun cloth carelessly thrown about the shoulders. A small black and white dog sat at his feet.

As he played I knew that the music was for me. The tune was different to the one that I had first heard, but was just as plaintive. Quietly I put down the scuttle, and descended the steps. As I moved towards the figure the music he played faded, and the outline of the apparition vanished; I was left cursing myself for the impetuosity of my nature.

A particular failing in me is my curiosity: I own to being both a gossip and a busybody, and yet for all that I wanted to discover the identity of the spectre, I was reluctant to tell anyone of my encounters with him. Thus I began to frequent public libraries, rummaging through old newspapers to find accounts of the building of the railway. There were no clues there on who the ghost could be. A strange flash of inspiration led me to explore a succession of country churchyards close to the railway and it was in the third of these that I discovered Irish Jack.

This discovery fuelled my curiosity even further. The enigmatic epitaph seemed to hint at further mystery. My thoughts were so much on Irish Jack that I allowed my romance of ten years standing to flounder, and my girl left me to marry the porter at Forncett.

A country signalman has an abundance of spare moments to brood over the events of his life. Most of my thoughts were directed towards the mystery of Irish Jack, and I spent many night-time hours at the window of my cabin willing him to reappear. But it is a known fact about apparitions that those attempting to seek them out will inevitably be disappointed. So it was with me now. Even on the most likely of nights nothing appeared. Weeks, months, a year passed without incident. Although my interest in Jack was still keen, he began to be less often in the forefront of my thoughts. Perhaps this device was intended to make his reappearance more welcome: certainly its spectacular manner was startling enough.

Horse Runs in Tring Cutting

The supernatural tableau was unfolded to me on a most inauspicious winter's night. A locomotive failure on my section had made life difficult early in the shift, with all traffic using the down line. The trouble was sorted out shortly before midnight, and as I put fresh water in my kettle I looked forward to an hour or so of relaxation before the ringing of the telegraph bell would again demand my attention.

It seemed no time at all before I dozed off, comfortably settled in the armchair close to the stove. Then, for no obvious reason, I felt fully awake. I glanced at the clock. Twenty minutes were all that had elapsed, yet subtle changes had occurred to my environment. The light bulb which illuminated my area of cabin was extinguished, and the one at the far end was giving out only a pathetic gleam. In sympathy with this, the fire in the stove had burned low: before my lapse into sleep its open door had given light from a cheerful blaze. But it was the scene that was revealed beyond the windows of the box which brought me fully to my senses, and set my heart beating powerfully. An unnatural, bluish, light gleamed through the glass, serving to show that the countryside had undergone an amazing change.

86

Much of the cutting away to my right had disappeared. Instead the hillside was being scarred by the activities of a hundred or so men who were working there. Some were emptying hods of earth into large wheelbarrows which were hitched to ropes to be pulled up the steep sides of this cutting-in-the-making. The men between the shafts of the wheelbarrows had to fight hard to keep the barrows on the narrow plankways as they were hauled to the top. As I watched one unfortunate fellow lost control of his overfilled barrow which left the planks and emptied its load over his sprawling body. After a moment he pushed himself free of the mud spoil, shouting to his mates to show that he had survived the accident.

Then I noticed a familiar figure sitting close to my viewpoint, which seemed to have escaped the straits of time. It was Irish Jack, his faithful terrier at his feet, who watched the activity going on around him in a detached way, an alien figure among those toiling so hard. A man at the head of the cutting (from his dress I guessed him to be the contractor or his overseer) shouted and waved his arms. Immediately work halted, and the navvies ran away from their excavation. Seemingly within seconds I saw puffs of smoke and then a great bank of earth collapsed as the dynamite achieved its purpose. It would have been unlucky for a man to stumble in his flight, for to do so would mean being ungulfed by a ton or more of earth which would take an hour to shift.

The movements of the workers now tended to suggest that this was the end of their toil for the day. Indeed, the strange light was by slow degrees turning from blue to ever-deeper shades of purple. Primitive huts lined the working, thatched with sacks, bracken and straw. To these the workmen retired, reappearing minutes later with steaming billy-cans to eat their dinners by the fires which burned outside the openings serving as doors. Now it was that Irish Jack got to his feet, and painfully dragged his gaunt body over to the glow of the fires. The navvies watched him suspiciously, their hard faces showing no hint of welcome. Tentatively he took the chanter of his pipes in his hands and inflated the bag with the bellows. Again I heard the sound of the lament he had played when I first saw him: it was as evocative of a deep sadness as it had been before – a longing for the heather-covered fastnesses of his own land so remote from the landscape of Norfolk.

The audience were now finishing their food, scrubbing at the bottoms of their billy-cans with enormous hunks of bread to remove the last drops of greasy stew. One by one they rose to their feet and

Builders of the Great Central

moved towards the lines of barrels placed by one of the huts, taking with them great quart tankards which they filled with ale. Effortlessly each man drained two of these measures, and then returned to the fireside.

Up to this time I had only been able to recognise general sounds, but now I realised that my senses were tuned to voices also. The piper was offered a can of food and paused in his playing to eat, greedily, throwing crusts and morsels to his dog. The largest, most brutal-looking of the navvies addressed him in a rich Yorkshire brogue:

'How does the work on the Shropshire Union fare? They say that he pays well, those that are left alive.'

'Surely,' answered Jack, 'if you care not what he makes you pay for scrag-end and a quart of porter. You fare better with your man here.'

From my experience in wartime I was able to identify the part of Ireland to which he was native. His voice belied his looks; it was rich and throaty, and bore the accent of the north of Ireland, Antrim or close by Belfast. The men seemed now to have accepted his presence, and ale was given him. The talk continued to discuss railway projects of the past with which I was unfamiliar. Some, said Jack, were tempted to work in France where pay was better and the contractors generally less rapacious.

Suddenly, out of the gloom, a new figure appeared. It was a young boy of nine or ten who was employed to lead the horses which transported the soil removed from the cutting. He approached timidly and in his hands held an object tightly wrapped in a soiled red handkerchief. He was asked roughly what business he had with the group. In answer, without speaking, he unwrapped an object from its covering. I could see, as it was brought to the light of the fire, that it was an article of rare beauty: although encrusted with dirt its shape showed through – it was a large medallion in the shape of a bird. Its body was a huge pearl, its wings were sparkling with small precious stones of every hue, and its golden talons held two larger stones, an emerald and a ruby.

'How did you come by this, boy?' asked the Yorkshireman.

The boy's voice was gentle, timid, broad Norfolk: 'Sir, it were just a-laying on the ground, by a great old puddle, up at the top.'

'It's a bauble, useless, worthless, but I could try to get you a penny or two for it from a man I know if you give it here.'

One or two of the other men exchanged wry winks and smiles at this offer.

'Oh no, sir, I like it too well. I be off to see my da tomorrow an' he'll be tickled to see this here.'

'Well you take care now not to lose it. Take yourself off to your bed; it's a long walk you'll have, come morning.'

The boy left the fireside and pushed through the sacking door of one of the huts. Irish Jack picked up his pipes again and resumed playing, a less melancholy air now, almost a jig, while the others chatted and obtained a different form of satisfaction from their own pipes, which gave off the thick, pungent fumes which come from the coarsest of plug tobaccos. Whether from previous experience, or from the remarkable vividness of the hallucination, I could clearly smell that aroma.

One by one the navvies left the warmth of the fire for their beds in the huts. Some just nodded at Jack as they retired (he had by this time finished his playing) others threw him a coin. He settled down for the night, pulling his rough cloak over his body. I knew how cold he must

The Great Central was the last major railway to be built in Britain

have been, even though the little dog was asleep in the curve of his body.

After a while (and I am unable to tell how long it was precisely, for in this strange, dream-like episode time seemed to have been telescoped) the boy returned to the fire, and threw sticks on it to revive its blaze. Carefully he unwrapped his beautiful treasure from its cloth, and turned it in the firelight, watching its coloured stones sparkle, as though they had an abundance of energy to release after being hidden for all those years. The boy had probably never had a toy in his life, or anything to truly call his own, and I felt the joy and wonder in him as he handled the priceless object.

However the boy's pleasure was to last for too short a moment: although my entire will was directed at warning him of the danger that was approaching, I was unable to utter a sound, or, indeed, even appear to any of the actors in the savage tableau that was being unfolded before me.

90

I saw two dark shapes emerge stealthily from a hut. They skirted the fire in order to come on the boy unseen, from behind. It was the big Yorkshireman and his crony, a balding, weasel-faced villain whom I had disliked at sight when I had seen him earlier. The fat man clasped a hand over the boy's mouth: his body convulsed, and then I saw the knife in the hand of the murderer as he wrenched it from the body. His accomplice picked up the fallen medallion. They were so intent on their business that they failed to notice that Jack, who had appeared a bundle on the ground some way distant from the fire, had awoken, and, his hand over the muzzle of his dog, had crept from the scene.

The Yorkshireman next took the medallion, wrapping it again in the blood-stained cloth that the boy had used. He was about to pocket it in his voluminous waistcoat when he noticed the abandoned blanket of the piper. He pointed at it to his accomplice, for a moment looking concerned, but then shrugged and whispered:

'So be it then, he may be the scapegoat. Go now to your rest and set off the hue and cry in his direction when the boy is discovered. Then make yourself scarce. We will meet as I said.'

This said, he made off into the darkness, while the rat-faced man silently disappeared into a hut.

A short time later, it seemed, the camp awoke. A dishevelled, unsavoury women emerged from the nearest hut, stretching and scratching herself. Even though it was still before dawn she was not long in finding the body of the boy, who lay where he had died. Her screams woke the rest of the workforce, and I noticed Rat-face was one of the first on the scene. It was he who pointed out the abandoned blanket of the piper, and the direction that the supposed murderer had taken. The navvies grabbed picks and shovels from the working and set off in pursuit, though it was noticeable that Rat-face kept to the rear of the throng.

Irish Jack, however, must have had his suspicions at the way that events were being directed. As the hue-and-cry disappeared into the distance he emerged from a hiding-place and began to make his way past the huts in the opposite direction, towards the head of the excavation. It was his misfortune that the harridan who had first raised the alarm should emerge from her hut at this moment and come face to face with, as she thought, the murderer.

Her screams were as powerful as they had been before, and arrested the navvies from their headlong pursuit. Jack had hoped to climb up the steep, muddy slope of the digging unobserved, but now that his whereabouts were betrayed he had no chance of doing this. Instead he stood his ground, trying to soothe the hysterical woman, obviously with the intention of proving his innocence to the angry workers.

However he was given no chance of doing this. The mob descended on him with their improvised weapons, and in seconds he was on the ground; his hands, at first upraised to protect his head, soon fell limp and bloody as his assailants increased their frenzy. I saw a flash of white as the dog ran around the ankles of the mob, nipping and biting. It was despatched by one swing of a shovel. As the terrible fury of the men became exhausted it began to snow – small flakes at first, but these rapidly grew in size until the whole scene was blotted out and I was magically returned to my cabin and my expected view of opaque darkness.

For days, weeks, following I pondered on my vision. I came to the conclusion that there must be further events that would eventually be shown to me. Otherwise how could the navvies have become enough reconciled to Irish Jack to subscribe to his grave? Of course they would find that the medallion was not concealed on his person, but would the real murderers ever be brought before the law? I was convinced that my dream had revealed the truth to me, but felt that there must be some business left undone: why else had the ghost appeared to me?

This time the answer was not long in coming. Conditions of climate seem to have served as a trigger again – this time for the final part of my supernatural sequence, or so I pray.

The night was wet as I trudged the lineside path to the box. It was cold, and on my way the rain turned to sleet, and by the time I arrived at the box, this had become snow. The last trains of the evening passed through. There was a long interval when I knew that no traffic was to approach the section, and so the bell would be quiet for a time. Again I settled to a gentle reverie in my armchair. Again I was transported to the landscape of the past.

On this occasion my eyes were directed into the wood at the top of the cutting. I could distinguish little at first, but at last the murky light revealed a man crouched, unnaturally, on the ground. It was the Yorkshireman, and I soon saw the reason for his strange posture – a man-trap had him by both legs. As I watched, his body keeled over, and I saw his grimace of pain as the jaws of the trap tore his flesh. I knew by the depth of snow around him, and by the amount of blood that had been spilled, that he had been trapped for some time. His shoulders shook with the agony of his predicament, and by the pallor of his face I could see that his final moments were approaching. With a final effort he raised himself on one arm and threw an object away from him. This accomplished he fell back, his face pressed hard to the snow.

I knew that the object was the medallion, and that I had seen a murderer suffering his just deserts: the cold would leave his body lifeless before the hour was out. My attendant spirit led my eyes to where the medallion fell. It was hidden between the convoluted roots of a venerable oak tree. I was allowed to dwell on the shape and aspect of the tree for a long moment before I realised that the increasing snowfall was about to blot out the image, and return me to my natural senses.

Now I asked myself for what purpose I had been given these details. I dwelt on the problem for some days before exploring the wood, which remained on either side of the cutting. It took but an hour or so to discover the oak whose roots concealed the medallion. It was in a state of decline, but its contorted base was as I remembered. With a trowel I carefully scraped at the accumulation of leaf-mould between the contorted roots. I was rewarded by first, a cloth wrapping and then by the brilliant sparkle of the gemstones of the medallion. Extracting it I felt the entrancement that it had held for the boy a century before.

As I look at it now, on the table in front of me, it retains its matchless beauty, and yet I begin to feel uneasy about the object. It's brilliance sometimes seems to be unworldly, its contours are not rhythmic in the way a craftsman would make them but seem to jar on the mind as well as the eye. I believe that the talisman has a significance that I do not understand, and that there may be ill fortune in it. After all it has brought about the death of three people that I know of: may I not be the fourth.

This is my purpose in relating the strange story. I am a lonely man and know few that will care much should I suffer an unnatural fate. But, finder, beware of the prospect of evil in the thing you will find wrapped in the stained cloth in my pocket.

The Strange Occurrence at the Victoria Hotel

My fondest memories of late childhood centre on the treasured occasions when I was invited to accompany my grandfather (on my mother's side) on one of his journeys. He was a traveller in 'printers' sundries', which covered a multitude of wares, and his journeys were mostly by train. He used a pony and trap to visit remote towns and villages not served by the railway. Grandfather's visits were eagerly awaited by customers in lonely villages, for he brought word of the news in the big world outside. In those days few newspapers reached beyond the major towns, and he was not only called upon to tell the news, but also interpret it – a task he thoroughly enjoyed, imposing his radical views on all and sundry, even arguing with customers of a different political persuasion.

The main purpose of my accompanying him was to carry his vast

A Great Eastern driver and fireman

A fenland junction

black umbrella above his head so that neither he, nor his precious samples, became spattered with rain. 'Hold that damned brolly up, boy,' he would shout, and this was no easy duty for a twelve-year-old boy, somewhat short for his age. I also helped load and unload his cases of wares, and it would be a long day for me, especially if there were calls to be made in the evening. Usually, though, the work ended about supper-time, when we would pull up at an old coaching-inn, or at a more modern 'commercial' hotel near the station.

There would always be a good company of travellers staying at these establishments; 'commercial gentlemen' who shared a large table at supper and provided their own amusements afterwards. By tradition, the most senior traveller present presided over these festivities and invariably my grandfather occupied this position. It was he who spoke the grace and carved the joint. Afterwards grandfather thanked their host and called upon all present to contribute a penny to the Widows' and Orphans' Fund and to preside over the 'kitty' that had been collected to pay for the evening's drinking (even teetotallers and those with late business elsewhere were expected to put into this).

95

I was never allowed to attend these functions, and indeed seldom had much inclination to do so, but on occasion, after I had eaten the supper brought to me in the room that I shared with my grandparent, I would be kept awake by the creakings of old timbers and by the unfamiliar shadows of a strange room. Then I would half-dress myself, and creep downstairs to a vantage point where I could watch the goings-on without being seen.

Sometimes these would hold little of interest to a young lad. Sing-songs were boring, and the noise kept me awake. So, too, were the occasions when each member of the company was called upon to perform his party-piece. These were often songs that were sung out of tune, or long monologues of absolute tedium. To me the highlight of the evening was the telling of ghost stories, with which it ended. These people were connoisseurs of the supernatural, and my grandfather told the best stories of all on these occasions. There was one in particular he related only once, after a specially convivial party, but he told it with such feeling that I can recall it almost word for word to this day.

It concerned one of the great hotels put up by the railway

Central Railway Station, Newcastle-upon-Tyne, opened 29 August 1850

companies close to their major stations: huge, pompous edifices that reflected the prosperity and confidence of the age in which they were built. It was not the sort of place normally used by grandfather, but on this occasion he was unable to obtain a room in the more humble hotel he usually stayed at, and so he had to settle for the splendours of the Victoria (he would never reveal its real identity, or even the town in which it was situated).

At this time electricity was being installed in hotels, but this had yet to reach the Victoria which still used gas-lamps. Its guests were able to use a lift (operated by hydraulic power) but the remainder of its comforts were old-fashioned. It could not, for example, boast that its bedrooms were heated by 'steam radiator'. Instead an army of maids had to drag coal-scuttles up and down the service stairs to tend the fires which burned in every occupied bedroom. Grandfather remembered one other idiosyncracy of the hotel: it claimed in advertisements: 'Importers of Live West Indian Turtle – turtle soup for dinner parties and invalids forwarded to any part of the country'. Such details remain in the mind long after more important matters are forgotten, yet I remember the phrase word-perfect from grandfather's preamble to his story.

Replete from a good supper, and not much caring for the company he found in the sitting-room or lounge, he went early to his room. There he found a blazing fire, and, after calling for a warming-pan to air his bed, retired and soon felt himself drifting into the deep first sleep of night.

But suddenly he was fully awake. No sound had disturbed him, yet in seconds he felt the atmosphere of the room change. The fire that had been burning so brightly now only glowed, sullenly. Instead of the usual creaks and groans of an old building, punctuated by the sounds of doors closing and raised voices, a deep and unnatural silence invaded the room. Then, by the drawn curtains, he perceived the dim outline of a figure. Slowly the outline of its form grew stronger and showed itself to be that of a woman. She held a handkerchief to her face and this may have stifled the sounds of her sobbing, which, he now saw, was racking her body.

A strange light was growing in intensity to illuminate the room more clearly: he saw different furnishings and articles of luggage and clothing to the ones that had been there before. Instead of his own shabby carpet-bag a great cabin-trunk stood by the far wall. Over it, he now saw, crouched a man. He was trying in a clumsy fashion to fold a leg, which protruded from the trunk, inside it so that he might close its lid. The foot wore a shoe of shiny patent leather; the man who was attempting to cram it into the trunk wore the uniform of a station porter. Each time he thought he had the foot successfully lodged inside the trunk, and made to close its lid, the leg would seem to twitch, and out it would spill again. At last he succeeded and by bouncing on the lid managed to secure the catches. For the first time the man's face was turned towards my grandfather. Already predisposed to see evil in it, he was still shaken by what he saw. It was a monster's face – a grotesque mask of irregular features, its left side further deformed by a hairy, warty excrescence of violent colours. It was contorted into an expression so hateful as to be hypnotic as he made for the door, the woman still sobbing by the window. Although the door had been left locked by grandfather, the creature opened it without a key, leaving it ajar. A moment later he returned, wheeling in a two-wheeled barrow on to which he loaded the trunk. With an abrupt gesture to the woman he left the room, pulling the barrow after him. A moment later the woman followed and the door closed, seemingly of its own accord, after them. As it closed the room seemed to come alive again. Now the usual sounds of hotel life could be heard; the fire burnt up brightly, its flames showing grandfather's familiar belongings strewn about as he had left them.

Not unnaturally grandfather admitted to being in a state of some perturbation at this point. After giving himself a brisk swig of brandy from the hip-flask that he always carried he put himself to rational thinking and came to the conclusion he had dreamed a particularly vivid nightmare – brought on, perhaps, by the rich fare he had supped earlier.

Sleep was not long in returning, but again, just as he hovered on its brink, the room turned chill and became bathed in the strange light just as before. The drama that unfolded, however, was not to be a continuation of the events he had witnessed previously; it soon became apparent that it concerned ones that had occurred at an earlier time.

The same woman was in the room, standing by the side of the table on which were laid documents and, it appeared, plans. Studying these were two men. One was of middle age, bearded and stoutly built, who leaned far over the table to regard the plans intently. The other was young, clean-shaven, and of striking good looks. He was removing a large neckerchief from his collar and having done so began to twist

Kilsby Tunnel under construction

it into a stout cord. His reason for doing so was quickly made plain. Some words he uttered caught the attention of the older man who looked up, his face showing bewilderment, sadness, and then anger, the emotions flickering across it like the clouds of a summer storm move across the face of the sun. Of an instant though the young man had the neckerchief knotted tight round the other's neck, his knee in the victim's back. The deadly cord was pulled taut across the windpipe. In vain, as his face purpled, he tried to thrust himself away from the table. In turns he scrabbled at the hands that held the garotte, then attempted to strike at the younger man who now stood behind him. The woman remained motionless throughout the minute or so that the struggle lasted, her face turned away. At last the victim's body slumped against that of the man who had so cruelly assaulted it, and he let it drop to the floor. He kneeled by its side, lifted a wrist and held it for a moment as though feeling for a pulse, and then gave a nod to the woman, attempting to smile at her, though his features refused to obey his will and instead made a ghastly grimace. The woman now came forward, and he saw that she was carrying a brown glass bottle upside-down, a large pad of cloth over its mouth. She passed the pad to her companion, who placed it over the face and mouth of his victim, turning his own face away. At that moment he revealed the left side of his face for the first time to the unseen witness. It bore a birthmark, grandfather realised, of the same shape that he had noticed in the previous dream – on the horrible face of the porter. This realisation seemed to dispel the nightmare: the figures faded, still locked in their embrace. The fire burned up again, the ghostly light faded, the normal illumination of the room again became the flickering flames of the fire.

This second episode succeeded in so disturbing grandfather's nerves that he slept no more that night. As he paid his account in the morning he asked the clerk whether anything untoward had ever occured in that room. The clerk replied that he was ignorant of any accident having taken place there and inquired whether grandfather had a particular reason for asking. The latter declined to give a reason for his request as he had determined to make further researches of his own which he wished to keep private.

One of his customers in that town was an old friend, and it was this man who provided the clue to the unravelling of the mystery. He was unable to shed light on a tragic incident in the hotel but added, as an afterthought, that there had been a tragedy at the station below some ten years before. He remembered that a husband, told of the infidelity of his wife, had laid himself in the path of a through express. His body had been so torn as to be unrecognisable, and though there had been suspicions about the wife's lover no evidence had been forthcoming to connect him with the husband's death.

Grandfather consulted the files of the local newspaper. Certainly the gutter Press had enjoyed themselves with the sensational affair.

100

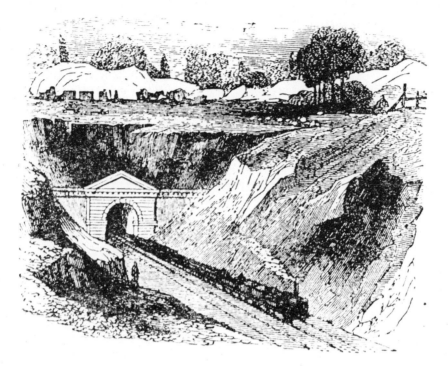

There were engravings of the protagonists at the inquest. All three
were recognisable as those who had acted out the dreams, though the
'murderer' appeared a handsome young man, not a disfigured
monster. In my grandfather's mind the events began to link up: the
confrontation, when the husband was told by his rival of his wife's
betrayal. Then the murder (for so it seemed), and the removal of the
body in the trunk. This was the clever touch, for no guest would give
a second glance to a porter wheeling a trunk through the hotel. A
covered way led directly to the platforms of the station and so it was
an easy business to choose a dark corner where the body could be
unloaded, and then left on the rails to be run over by the through
express.

But why, in the first dream, had the porter's face appeared so
hideous? Certainly it could not have been thus at the time the events
took place, for such a face would have been remembered by anyone
who had encountered it, and the birthmark had convinced my

grandfather that the murderer and the evil porter were one and the same person. He was compelled to investigate further.

By good fortune (and by his own thoughtful inquiries) he was able to discover the movements of the couple after the notoriety of the affair had died down. He was helped in this by the fact that a considerable fortune had been left to the wife at the death of her husband. He learned from a garrulous servant that they had indeed married; the murderer being her cousin. The marriage had been a hasty affair, for the wife was already pregnant with her lover's child and wished it to be born in wedlock (a strange sentiment for one who had executed such evil designs in getting her way). Grandfather was told that the woman had died at the birth of her child, which was stillborn. Its father took to drink and laudanum after the death of his wife. His features became disfigured, his form hunched and unnatural. At the last he was committed to a padded cell at the County Asylum. There he survived only a short time, endlessly shrieking the same words: 'See, the train will get you, the train will get you.'

It was these words that ever afterwards puzzled my grandfather. Had he witnessed the murder in his dream, or was it accomplished by the wheels of the Scottish express?

The Monster of the Marshes

I have always been a romantic, even when I was mad. Insanity is a strange illness; when it is coming on all your relations and friends sense it, but the person suffering from it goes about his everyday life normally, as he thinks. Of course, looking back the symptoms were all there. Some of them may have been dismissed as youthful eccentricity, but there is no getting away from the effect that my outlandish dress and manners made at that time. I wore my hair long (something that few other young men did in the 1950s) and affected flowing cloaks and wide-brimmed, floppy hats. I believed that the light of genius was in my eyes, but most probably it was the light of madness. I made a great thing of my artistic temperament, and when I had a short, ostentatious poem published by an obscure magazine my vanity knew no bounds. All this was tolerated for a time by those I knew and loved, but over the course of a few months my behaviour deteriorated. I drank heavily, became violent, and hurt all those who I loved. After a particularly vicious episode I was persuaded to go to

Norwich (Thorpe) c. 1912

see the family doctor, who in turn sent me to a psychiatrist who advised a voluntary stay in hospital 'for my own good'.

There I broke down completely. I allowed the side of my nature that I had been fighting to take me over. For the best part of a year I was utterly withdrawn into myself. As the crisis receded I regained a part of my former personality, but was convinced that this was only a period of remission and that soon I would lapse again to become a stranger to myself. I decided to kill myself at the first opportunity.

Having taken this decision I spent months brooding over the method I would use. This speeded my recovery as it gave me an aim in life, as it were. Not that I had an abundance of choice. Although by now I was supposed to be a voluntary patient at the institution, voluntary had little meaning in this context. It is true that I was allowed out on days when I was not undergoing treatment, but these moments of freedom were brief. Certainly I could not have gone about the shops in the village buying quantities of aspirin, for this would immediately have aroused the suspicions of the shopkeepers who knew very well where I came from. As a romantic I felt that death by hanging was squalid, undignified, and hard to achieve. I still prided myself on my looks and did not want to be found with mottled complexion and protruding tongue.

Eventually I narrowed it down to two choices: I could drown myself or throw myself beneath the wheels of a train. I dithered between the two. On my afternoon walks I was compulsively drawn to the railway, and to the marshes and river beyond. On some days I liked the idea of my wan corpse being discovered floating in the river, features composed and tranquil, like the Lady of Shallot. At other times I visualised the terrible moment of panic after the chilling plunge, weed clutching at my limbs as I breathed the choking liquid for the first time. Then I found that the city's sewerage outfall was just above the place I had chosen for my death and so this scheme was abandoned.

This left the railway. The chief reason against this was its messiness, and although I liked the drama of the scene, I hated to inconvenience people and could imagine the repugnance that the ambulance-men would feel confronted by a mangled corpse strewn along a hundred yards or so of track. On the other hand I believed that it should be possible to arrange for the death to happen tidily, if care were taken. Anyway I had always loved trains, another characteristic of the romantic.

Fog at Norwich

It was dusk when I set out on what I intended should be my last walk. I had gone out on the excuse that I needed an urgent money order, otherwise I would certainly not have been allowed out so late. It seemed an ideal night for my purpose. A shallow mist was rising from the marshes so that the bodies of the cattle grazing there looked as though they were floating like balloons above the ground. Yet the mist was not so dense that it would delay the trains, for the cabs of the engines would be above it and the drivers able to see the signals clearly. However they would never see my body lying on the track.

I came to the crossing and opened the gate. There was no one about at all, the track only went to a handful of bungalows and a couple of boatyards, almost deserted at this time of year. I walked on the sleepers for about a quarter of a mile until I was almost opposite the home signal. My train was the 4.20 from Norwich to Yarmouth. I took off my cloak, rolled it up, and placed it as a cushion close to the outside rail. Then I took a lingering look at the darkening landscape

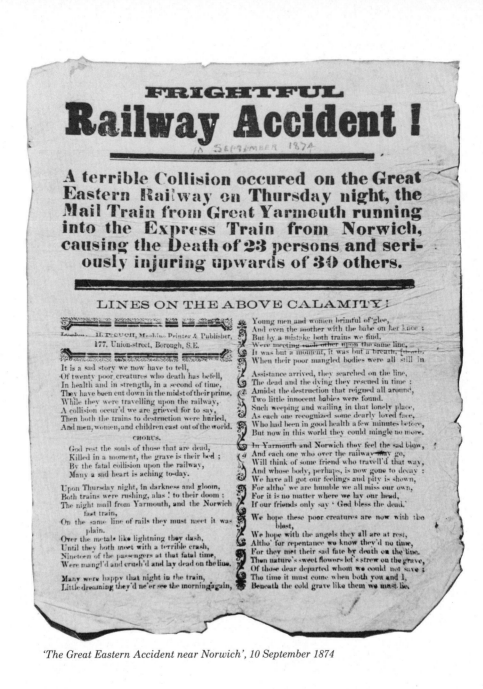

FRIGHTFUL
Railway Accident !

In September 1874

A terrible Collision occured on the Great Eastern Railway on Thursday night, the Mail Train from Great Yarmouth running into the Express Train from Norwich, causing the Death of 23 persons and seriously injuring upwards of 30 others.

LINES ON THE ABOVE CALAMITY!

London.—H. Disley, Machine Printer & Publisher, 177, Union-street, Borough, S.E.

It is a sad story we now have to tell,
Of twenty poor creatures who death has befell,
In health and in strength, in a second of time,
They have been cut down in the midst of their prime,
While they were travelling upon the railway,
A collision occur'd we are grieved for to say,
Then both the trains to destruction were hurled,
And men, women, and children cast out of the world.

CHORUS.

God rest the souls of those that are dead,
Killed in a moment, the grave is their bed ;
By the fatal collision upon the railway,
Many a sad heart is aching to-day.

Upon Thursday night, in darkness and gloom,
Both trains were rushing, alas ! to their doom :
The night mail from Yarmouth, and the Norwich fast train,
On the same line of rails they must meet it was plain.
Over the metals like lightning they dash,
Until they both meet with a terrible crash,
Nineteen of the passengers at that fatal time,
Were mangl'd and crush'd and lay dead on the line.

Many were happy that night in the train,
Little dreaming they'd ne'er see the morning again,

Young men and women brimful of glee,
And even the mother with the babe on her knee :
But by a mistake both trains we find,
Were meeting each other upon the same line,
It was but a moment, it was but a breath, forsooth,
When their poor mangled bodies were all still in death

Assistance arrived, they searched on the line,
The dead and the dying they rescued in time :
Amidst the destruction that reigned all around,
Two little innocent babies were found.
Such weeping and wailing in that lonely place,
As each one recognized some dearly loved face,
Who had been in good health a few minutes before,
But now in this world they could mingle no more.

In Yarmouth and Norwich they feel the sad blow,
And each one who over the railway may go,
Will think of some friend who travell'd that way,
And whose body, perhaps, is now gone to decay :
We have all got our feelings and pity is shown,
For altho' we are humble we all miss our own,
For it is no matter where we lay our head,
If our friends only say ' God bless the dead.'

We hope these poor creatures are now with the blest,
We hope with the angels they all are at rest,
Altho' for repentance we know they'd no time,
For they met their sad fate by death on the line.
Then nature's sweet flowers let's strew on the grave,
Of those dear departed whom we could not save :
The time it must come when both you and I,
Beneath the cold grave like them we must lie.

'The Great Eastern Accident near Norwich', 10 September 1874

106

THE FATAL RAILWAY ACCIDENT NEAR NORWICH

July 14th, 1846.

NORFOLK RAILWAY.

Miles.	Stations.	DOWN TRAINS.							SUNDAY TRAINS.				
		A.M.	A.M.	A.M.	A.M.	P.M.	P.M.	MAIL.	A.M.	A.M.	A.M.	P.M.	MAIL
0	LONDON	....	....	8 0	11 30	....	5 0	8 40	....	....	6 45	2 0	8 3
57¼	CAMBRIDGE	....	7 0	10 38	1 46	....	7 38	11 26	....	7 0	9 48	5 11	11 20
88	BRANDON	....	8 22	12 0	3 0	....	9 0	12 49	....	8 22	11 13	6 25	12 1
95½	THETFORD	....	8 34	12 14	3 14	....	9 14	1 10	....	8 34	11 30	6 37	1 10
103½	Harling Road	....	8 46	12 26	3 26	....	9 26	....	....	8 46	11 42	6 48	....
106¼	Eccles Road	....	8 54	12 34	....	....	9 34	....	....	8 54	11 50	6 56	....
110	ATTLEBOROUGH	....	9 7	12 47	3 41	....	9 47	1 45	....	9 7	12 6	7 11	1 1
113	Spooner Row	....	9 12	12 52	....	....	....	....	....	9 12	12 11	7 15	....
115½	WYMONDHAM	....	9 27	1 5	1 0	....	10 5	1 58	....	9 27	12 26	7 29	1 5
119½	Hethersett	....	9 33	....	....	....	....	....	....	9 33	12 32	7 34	....
125	Trowse	....	10 2	....	1 30	....	....	....	....	10 2	1 2	8 2	....
...	...... Carrow	....	10 7	1 42	4 35	....	10 37	2 38	....	10 7	1 7	8 7	2 2

around me. I could just see the lights of the village on the rising ground away from the river. Mist hid the station about half a mile up the track – Whitlingham. I remember thinking ironically how appropriate that was – the scene of the worst railway disaster in Norfolk's history – when two trains met on a single track and twenty-five people were killed.

With a sudden clatter the signal-arm fell. My train was on time. I heard it whistle at the crossing by Thorpe Gardens. I knew that it would not stop at Whitlingham and so knelt down on the track, bowing my neck to the rail. This position was by no means comfortable, though the folded cloak gave some support. I felt rather than heard the train's approach. Although I had intended to watch its relentless rush towards me, at the last moment I turned my head away. I was confronted, in the dusky light, about a yard from my face, by the most hideous features I had ever encountered. It was the face of a monster, a ghastly mask hanging disembodied in the mist. Its lips curled back and mouth opened in a soundless snarl. I could see an array of sharp-pointed scarlet fangs, and the thing's breath stank of the evil of death.

With a scream I threw myself away from the creature, and away from the train which passed within inches of my body. I lay prone for a number of minutes, panting for breath, my heart kicking at the walls of my chest. I hardly dare open my eyes to see whether the fiendish thing was still there. I could imagine it sniffing at my face, and smelt again its foetid breath which, real or imagined, turned my stomach. At last I summoned the courage to open my eyes. Darkness had fallen abruptly and now I could see nothing beyond the dull sheen of the rails. Trembling still I rose to my feet, brushed down my clothes, picked up the cloak, and returned to the hospital.

Recently, to a very few of my personal friends, I have been able to tell this story against myself. I was even able to provide a rational explanation for the monster. Could it have been one of the first coypu to have invaded Norfolk? These hideous-looking rat-like creatures, as big as a medium-sized dog, were later to become the deadly enemies of marshland farmers, but at that time they were largely unknown. Although I can make out a convincing case for this explanation there is something in me which will never believe it. My crisis of personality had been cured by the encounter. My psychiatrist (who was not told the story) was amazed by the suddenness of my recovery. I had managed to rid myself of the Mr Hyde part of my personality, and my Dr Jekyll-self was never again troubled by a dual nature. Occasionally my meeting with my own personal devil has been re-enacted in a nightmare and then, awaking sweating and trembling, I know that I have seen a real image of Hell, but have escaped from the Devil sent to pursue me there.

The earliest railway station at Norwich, 1862

The Platform Dog

Even in the heyday of steam there were not many people at our station to greet the arrival of the newspaper train at 3.27 a.m. As a very junior member of the staff of the goods depot, it often happened that this thankless task fell to me, and I had to help the guard offload the bundles of papers from the van and then cart them to the ramp where the wholesaler's vehicles were waiting. When this had been done the station closed for the night – only for a couple of hours, in truth, but nearly all the lights were extinguished, and if you were unfamiliar with its layout, it became a dangerous as well as a sinister place to be. Perhaps management had decided on this course of action to discourage the usual gathering of down-and-outs so frequently to be found in stations at night. Anyway I was left alone there, cleaning lamps and doing other insignificant jobs until my relief signed on at

'Help' – the Railway Dog of England and Travelling Agent for the Orphans of Railwaymen who were killed on duty

6.30. There should have been a copper patrolling the premises too, but most nights he found a haven of warmth, light and, perhaps, booze elsewhere so I was usually left on my own.

From the first I had made myself comfortable for this duty in a disused room in the Goods Office. There I had a disintegrating armchair, a blazing fire with a kettle forever on the hob (in those days drivers would always let you 'borrow' a pailful of coal from their bunkers), and a green-shaded light which enabled me to get an early look at the news. Where many might have found the solitude wearisome, I enjoyed it, and actually looked forward to these occasions.

Not so my colleague who was to do the turn on opposite weeks to me. He started with the railway after me, and when I relieved him after his first night-time shift I found him huddled in the old armchair, white as the proverbial sheet. The fire was burnt right down and his eyes were wide in terror, staring at the door that I had just unlocked and opened.

'Blast me, Boy, you look like you've seen a ghost,' I said, without being at all original.

'So I have, man, and I tell you I'm doing no more of this.'

As he spoke he got unsteadily to his feet and I thought at first he had been drinking, until he came closer and I found there was no smell of it on his breath. He was shaking, either with cold or fright, and seemed to have taken on many years overnight. The day previous he had been a carefree lad of sixteen. Now he had the bearing of an old man.

I crossed the room, stirred up the fire, and heaped coals on it. I noticed that the kettle was still full, the teapot had not been used. Had I been on duty I would have emptied the pot twice in that time. Whatever it was that had upset the boy, it had certainly succeeded in making him ignore the comforts of life.

'So,' I said, 'you've had a dream, have you? The governor wouldn't be much pleased to know you've had two hours kip on the Company. Anyway, I reckon a nightmare serves you about right, mate, specially when there's a dozen lamps to clean and the sheets to be made out.'

'It were no nightmare, Todd,' (my name being Sweeney, this had been a natural name for me since infancy); 'I tell you in God's truth there's a ghost in this place and I'm not stopping here to meet it twice.'

By now I had got the fire to rights, and the kettle had begun to sing. I stopped myself from calling him a bloody fool and made the pot of tea. As I handed him his mug, scalding, and sweet with the lashing of condensed milk, I asked him what had occurred.

He had seen off the newspaper train, and then gone back to the ramp to help load the two vans. Then he went to the cubby-hole by the Station Master's office where the main switches were installed. As he clicked off the last switch he thought he saw a shape move by the platform barrier. Without putting on any of the lights again, he took up his lantern and, not unduly worried, cautiously moved forward to investigate, even though he felt almost certain that his imagination had tricked him. Then he saw two eyes watching him. They were luminous, yellow, and stared without blinking, as big as saucers. Again he shone his lantern in that direction – the eyes vanished, yet without the illumination they appeared again, as baleful and disturbing as before. The boy remained cool enough to return to the switches, only a few steps away, and he flicked as many down as he could with one movement, so that the station was immediately lit brightly once again. Just as he did so he felt something brush past the legs of his trousers yet the lights showed the platforms, waiting-rooms and offices to be absolutely deserted. He quickly walked to the corner where he had seen the eyes, expecting to discover pieces of glass or other material there that would have reflected the light of his lantern. There was nothing at all to account for his experience.

He extinguished the lights again, swung his lantern high, and began to walk back to the warmth of his fire at the Goods Office. Suddenly he was nudged at the back of the knees. He recognised the sensation – it was the nudge usually delivered unerringly by a dog's nose when he wants to draw your attention to something. Instinctively he glanced behind and immediately saw again those yellow, saucer eyes. Shrieking, he turned the beam of the lantern on them. They vanished. He ran to our haven in the Goods Office, locked both the doors, and sat himself down by the fire, which though well stacked with good coal, burnt only dimly. And there he remained until I found him two hours later. Even though jobs were hard to come by, he gave in his notice the same day, and his friends told me that he was never the same man again, but always seemed to live frightened, and had to be locked away for his own good before he was twenty-five.

For the rest of the week I agreed to take the night shift. After the departure of the newspaper train on the night following I felt a little unease, yet after I had put out the lights nothing untoward happened, and I concluded that the incidents described to me by my unhappy

'Tim' – who between 1892 and 1902 collected at Paddington Station upwards of £800 for the GWR Widows and Orphans Fund

colleague were the imaginings of a deluded brain. Our perception is not always perfect: temperament and physical agencies inside and outside the body can distort things that we are convinced we have seen, and I believed that I was being charitable in discounting his supernatural explanation.

It was the events that occurred on the Saturday night that altered my opinions. Again, the last train had departed and the vans had gone with the Sunday newspapers. I turned off the lights and prepared to leave the station, for on the Sabbath there were no early trains, the first leaving just before noon. As I walked through the station, taking care to keep away from the edge of the platform, I experienced my first psychic feeling. *I knew that I was not alone.* I stopped, and raised my lantern. Of course there was nothing to be seen, and so I continued on my way. As I did so I realised that it was the soft, padding footsteps of a dog that had put me on my guard: now I could also hear the panting of his breath. Not unmindful of the lad's experiences I peered around me, searching for the yellow, saucer eyes. There was nothing to be seen, but all of a sudden I felt the gentle nudge of a nose at the back of the knee, just as had been described.

'Bugger off, you daft brute,' I shouted, and that is exactly what the spectral hound did. I heard him pad, pad, away from me, and I shone the lantern towards the sound, but of course there was nothing to be seen.

After this I was rarely bothered by the animal. On occasions I sensed his presence, but was never frightened for now I knew that I had control over him, just as my own dog obeyed me. I even came to be disappointed if the creature was not there, for I felt that he was not an unhappy ghost, but a creature who craved human affection and company, and I believe that during my brief stay at the station I was able to provide him with this.

It was many years later that I discovered an explanation for the animal's ghostly presence. I had been sent on a course to London, and met up with a man of my native town who I had not seen for many years. After several pints one evening I told him the story: I had never said anything of it before, not even to my wife. He listened intently, and when it was finished said, 'You know, the dog was called Bristol Bob. I heard my grandfather, who worked on that line, speak of him when I was a child. He used to be led around the station with a collecting-box on his back, for charity. There were dogs like that at most important stations, and they became very famous and earned charities a great deal of money. There was one called London Jack at, I think, Waterloo, who was a great favourite with Queen Victoria. When he died he was stuffed and put in a glass case at the station. I think he ended up at Southampton, but he wasn't there when I last looked. Bristol Bob was never stuffed, but he was there for many years and was a lovely old fusspot, apparently. But he could never have been a malicious ghost – he was too gentle a creature. It sounds as though your mate must have done something to upset him: why, with his "saucer eyes" he sounds more like Black Shuck, and, you know, if you look back at that one you're dead within the year. But, then, you're still alive so it couldn't have been him, could it?'

So the mystery remained. Why was the dog, harmless to me, so lethal to my young colleague? Was there a latent streak of evil in him which was recognised by the dog? Certainly it was his meeting with the dog that caused his downfall, and I learnt later that he spent his last years in the asylum incessantly shouting at the animal which, indeed, had frightened him out of his wits.

The Jinxed Jubilee

Steve Banyard went to a lot of trouble to make his visit to the remote scrapyard siding, and he was uncertain of his motives in making the trip. Had he gone to gloat over a corpse in decay, or was there something in him that could not bear the thought of *Lynx* disappearing from the face of the earth without him paying her his last respects? He had recognised her at once, among the crowd of derelicts in similar condition. Her nameplate had gone, but the number was still on the cab: 45743, below it a crudely painted letter 'C', standing for 'condemned'. Even in this shabby state the engine remained distinctive; for Steve she had an aura of sinister fascination that was unique. Nor would he have been unduly surprised to see her come suddenly to life, and steam off down the rusty tracks towards the main line.

Steve had been at great pains to learn every detail of her history. He had found that from the first she had been unlucky. In the mid 1930s,

Barry scrapyard

The Blitz, Camden Marshalling Yard, by Norman Wilkinson

while under construction at Crewe, a crane had dropped a large piece of her superstructure, killing a foreman. Soon after, while still being run in, she had hit a cart on a farm crossing. Again the accident had been fatal, this time to the farmhand. A little later she was successful in helping two suicide attempts succeed – separate occasions, these, to the famous double suicide she aided much later when her bogie wheels put an end to the earthly sufferings of a celebrated actor-manager and his boy-friend.

There had been a couple of further incidents during the war. At the height of the raids on Coventry *Lynx* found herself at the station there; the fireman made off for the air-raid shelter, but the driver decided to stay with his train, taking refuge beneath the engine. A land-mine exploded about fifty feet away, and though *Lynx* suffered little damage, being screened by another train, so great was the blast at ground-level that the driver's lungs were burst and he died almost instantly.

By this time the crews were becoming wary of the locomotive. They re-christened her 'Jinx' after this last incident, and attributed every little misfortune to the curse that they believed had been laid on her.

117

A pristine 'Jubilee', Achilles

However the worse was yet to come, though in this next accident she was not to suffer harm herself.

The mishap occurred in the final months of the war, when six years of hard use, and a somewhat neglected maintenance programme, had contributed to make much of the motive power available unreliable, to say the least. *Lynx*'s right-hand coupling-rod came adrift when she was at the head of fifty refrigerated meat-vans, descending a one-in-a-hundred gradient. Of course the crew immediately shut off steam and applied the brakes once they felt the uneven running and saw ballast flying past the window of the cab, but by then the damage had been done. The sleepers of half a mile of track had been disturbed, and from the opposite direction the Heysham–Euston boat-train was approaching. Fortunately the gradient meant that this was labouring at about forty miles an hour, but its engine became derailed as it passed *Lynx* and turned over as it ploughed into the meat-vans. The leading

118

Not so pristine; 45637 Windward Islands *after the Harrow disaster, 15 October 1952*

coaches telescoped and within half a minute a terrible scene had been created, human and animal carcasses intermingled. Twenty died in the accident, and fifty or so more were seriously hurt.

Nationalisation saw *Lynx* in new livery, but her troubles continued, albeit not to such a blood thirsty degree as before. She now seemed to enjoy making life hell for those who had to work with her. If she were derailed, then you could be sure that it would be at the 'throat' of a busy station. She once succeeded in closing down Euston altogether during the rush-hour. If she was going to run out of steam, then you could bet that it would be in the middle of an unventilated tunnel. Driver and fireman would have to crouch on the floor of the cab, or drop to the tracks, to breathe deep lungfuls of relatively clean air while the fire burned up. All the crews at the shed were anxious to avoid working her with the exception of Steve Banyard who, for some reason he failed to understand, enjoyed her perversity, and was determined to tame her. Later he would boast that his success was due to his treating her like he would a woman, with just the right amount of indifference mixed with extra care at difficult times.

Anyway, his treatment proved successful, and *Lynx* seldom got herself into trouble. Whereas before it had been difficult to persuade firemen to work her, they began to forget their prejudices and, since Steve was a good driver and companion, volunteered for duties with her. Steve knew that the engine was still capable of throwing tantrums, but he felt himself to be in control of her, and prided himself on this.

By now the days of steam were drawing to an end. Like most enginemen of the time Steve resented the coming of the diesels but had to resign himself to working with them. His last trip with *Lynx* was a sad one, and he felt a strong surge of affection as he left her for the last time, in the siding by the ash-pits. Her last steam hissed gently from the leaky joints, her last smoke drifted peacefully up to the dusky sky. Steve thought he would never see her in steam again.

But he was mistaken in thinking this. Shortly after his sad visit to the scrapyard, he read that *Lynx* had been bought by the Cwm Avon Steam Trust – a preservation society situated in the valleys of South Wales. They intended to restore her to her former glory immediately, and hoped to have the work done in time to have her in steam for the start of the summer season. However this forecast proved to be over-optimistic, and when Steve travelled to Cwm Avon late that summer he found her still in the workshop – in small pieces. Members of the society that he spoke to were fascinated to learn that he had been their engine's last driver, and eagerly questioned him about her characteristics in steam, but Steve refrained from telling them the less savoury details of her history, and left for home feeling flattered by the attention he had received.

Lynx took to the rails again the summer following. Her inaugural run was a fête day for Cwm Avon and attracted a great deal of Press and television coverage. Steve was working that day, otherwise he would have attended, but he was able to view brief moments on TV.

The Minister of State for Welsh Affairs cut the ribbon in front of *Lynx*'s buffers. It would have been in character for her to have promptly run him over, to share the fate of the unfortunate Mr Huskisson at the opening of the Liverpool & Manchester Railway. This was not to be, however. Instead there was a dramatic pause while the crowds waited for *Lynx* to draw majestically forwards. But

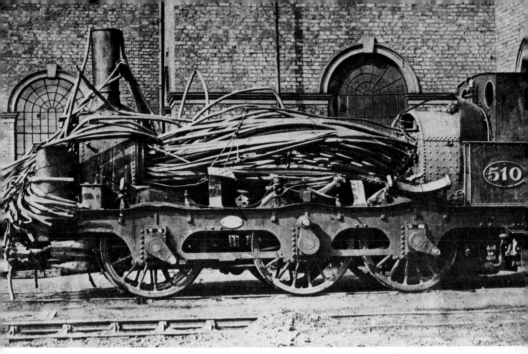

NER loco No. 510 after a boiler explosion 28 March 1877. The driver and fireman were both unhurt

nothing happened, until the red-faced driver emerged from his cab to announce that nothing he could do would get the brake off. For the rest of the afternoon the recalcitrant engine stood immobile at the platform as an army of amateur mechanics attempted to dismantle the mechanism. In the end her fire had to be dropped where she stood, and there she remained until the week-end following when a mechanic familiar with her class was brought to Cwm Avon and eventually put her right.

Lynx's reluctance to begin a new career did not end with this incident. She never steamed properly, even for the three and a half mile run to Pontfadog. She particularly resented having to make the return journey tender-first. Having run round her train she would approach it again forwards. Coupling-up this way round proved to be a nightmare for her driver. Suddenly the controls seemed to be ridiculously sensitive. Beckoned onwards by his fireman he would inch closer and closer to his coaches, yet however delicately he did this the locomotive would suddenly surge forwards at the last, so that there would be an unholy clash of buffers and often bumps and bruises for the passengers.

Yet no one could blame *Lynx* for the final disaster. Amateur engineers can be remarkably clever in getting results after by-passing regular procedures. They may, however, occasionally engage in irresponsible enterprises which can prove extremely dangerous. A group of these gifted amateurs decided to improve her steaming by modifying the blastpipe, etc. When the alterations were complete, it was decided that she should be tried out on the following Sunday – the very day that Steve had elected to visit her again at Cwm Avon.

A fire had been kindled and had got going nicely when the group of would-be Stephensons took themselves off to the pub, confident that there would be a good working pressure on the gauge when they returned.

Steve turned up at about half past two to find the place deserted. He let himself into the old engine-shed which was the Trust's headquarters. There he found *Lynx*, steam hissing viciously out of every pipe and crevice. He climbed up to the footplate and glanced at the dial: the needle was jammed up against the stop – well over 350 lb. Desperately, he reached for the knobs to release some of the pressure, turned them, but there was no effect. At that moment the boiler exploded. The force of the explosion de-roofed the engine-shed and destroyed most of the rolling-stock standing near by. It also decimated the executive members of the Trust who had just at that moment returned from the pub. Steve's body had been hurled back against the bulkhead of the tender, and, already lifeless, it was then disintegrated by the force and heat of the escaping steam. The black curse laid on *Lynx* from the time of her building had at last been dispelled – by her own destruction.

Privett Tunnel

My story concerns the Meon Valley line, from Alton to Fareham, which was one of the last railways to be built in England; it was still incomplete at the turn of the century. As a young lad my father was one of the carters engaged to take away the spoil from the cuttings and tunnels, but he was killed in the First World War so I can hardly remember him. I worked on the line for most of my life, first for the London & South Western, and then later for the Southern. When Nationalisation came I carried on for a few more years, but in the end they wanted to send me off to Southampton and I quit then. There had been a kind of glory in being a railwayman before, but once it became British Railways, and with steam thrown out of the windows, everything about it seemed to become shabby and lacklustre – all the old romance and loyalties were lost.

My mother, my elder sister and I lived in a cottage on the Basing estate, close to Privett. When I left school I was lucky to join the railway: jobs were scarce then and usually positions were only given to those who had relatives already employed with the Company. However my 'Uncle', who came to live with us after my father was killed in Flanders, worked for a large firm of corn-merchants. He had occasion to use the Meon Valley line for the carriage of a considerable quantity of grain each year. Consequently he put in a good word for me and at the age of fourteen I joined the permanent-way gang. After five or six years with them, and with my shoulders and back well strengthened by the heaving, shovelling and lifting, I was asked to be a linesman, and was responsible for about ten miles of track north of West Meon. Here the line climbs steeply through the chalky downs, diving into long tunnels at West Meon, and soon afterwards at Privett.

I never cared for either of these tunnels very much. They were dismal holes, and even though there was ventilation, smoke lingered perpetually, and sooty water was always dripping from the slimy roof. Sometimes, when forced to use one of the refuges because of a passing train, you would disturb a colony of bats, which would put the fear of God into you by silently fluttering through your hair, gently brushing against your face. If you put out your hand to steady yourself you might encounter damp, noxious fungus or embryonic stalactites. On an early occasion of my having to use a refuge I had put my hand upon

Watford Tunnel, 1837

the fur of a long-dead, mouldy, fox, which had obviously used the tunnel to escape from the hounds and then been struck down by a train. Once you began to think of the evil things that could dwell in these unlit, smoky caverns there was no end to it, and many men refused stretches of line with tunnels in them, saying that they suffered from claustrophobia and were unable to work in confined spaces. In fact I found out that my predecessor had made such an excuse to rid himself of this stretch of line, but only later did I begin to suspect that this was not his true reason for quitting.

I did not like either of my two tunnels much, but of the two the one beneath Filmore Hill, at Privett, was by far the worst. There was something about it which made me put off going through it unless I was forced to work there. Although the direct route home after working on the northern section of my line was through the tunnel, I seldom walked along the track, preferring to climb over the hill in the fresh air, enjoying the countryside and a sight of the sky. The beauty of this helped me forget the depressing gloom of the place beneath my feet.

Yet I still had to venture there sometimes – to check the fishplates,

125

On the Southern – West Meon Station

track-bed, drains and so on. You could walk about half a mile in from the southern end and still see daylight, but then the line curved and for some way you would be in total darkness. One day, in early autumn, I was busy in the dark there, trying to channel off water from a leaky bit of brickwork. I stopped shovelling the ballast for a moment, my senses distracted by what I thought I had heard. The silence was, indeed, imperfect. I heard the sound of singing for the first time – not the singing of the rails which warns of an oncoming train, but the sound of a man's voice, unaccompanied. It came from nowhere in particular, but echoed down the long murky corridor. It was singing a hymn – 'Rock of Ages' I think it was, that first time.

'Hello, you there,' I shouted, 'where are you? You'd best look out. There's a train due shortly.'

The singer did not seem to hear my words. He went on with the hymn as though there had been no interruption, and continued to its end, which coincided with the passage through the tunnel of the morning pick-up goods from Fareham. When this had passed all was quiet again; I might as well have been in my grave, except for the random drips and splashes of water leaking through the brick lining.

126

I hurried to the end of my task at that place, and was glad to be able to think of other urgent duties elsewhere, out of the tunnel, which could occupy me for the remainder of the day.

Soon afterwards I was again seconded to a permanent-way gang for a short time. During this stint I had to visit Winchester to collect materials. In the canteen there I met Jack Monkton, the linesman who had tended Privett Tunnel before me. He was a gaunt man, old before his time. I only realised that he had been my predecessor when the talk turned to the weird or ghoulish happenings that had occurred in the past on the railways of the district. A fireman was telling of the German airman who had fallen from a Zeppelin to land in a soft meadow alongside the 'Sprat and Winkle' at Mottisfont.

'Left an impression four feet deep, he did. You could see that he hit the ground spreadeagled-like, and then he bounced. We were sent with a van to pick up what bits we could find. They say that every year after, on that same night, he falls again, and screams all the way down.'

There was a pause while we digested this grisly story, then the cadaverous permanent-way man spoke:

'You'll find worse than that in Privett Tunnel, any of you what's fool enough to look.'

My mates all looked at me, but I shook my head at them and they kept quiet.

'I doubt that anyone could work down that hell-hole for long and keep sane. It's bad enough without the thing that lives there, but it were that what turned me off in the end. I couldn't stick it.'

He looked round, obviously waiting for encouragement to continue his story. A young engine-cleaner, with a grin at the rest of us, asked him to tell what happened.

'It's an evil place, that tunnel, at the best of times. I'd never hang about there long if I could help it, but one time I had to spend three or four days there patching brickwork. At first I had a mate along to help, but he only lasted a day. He reckoned he put his back out, though he hadn't been happy working there just the one day, even with me there with him. We kept hearing things, we thought. Sounds which weren't natural in a place like that.

'The first day that I was down there on my own it was even worse. There were noises like the creaking of timbers, earth slithering, and distant voices. Twice I walked through to where the sounds seemed to be coming from, by a ventilation shaft, but couldn't see anything.

127

I reckoned it was lads playing tricks, but there didn't seem much sense in it, and they didn't tire of their game in a hurry: it went on all day, and by the finish they were singing hymns.'

I was tempted to tell him of my experiences at this point, but obviously he had more to tell so I held my peace. He went on:

'The next day it was even worse. Things kept crashing down from on top, and I thought "I'll put a stop to them beggars" and climbed up over the hill to the shaft where the noise was coming from. I came on it stealthy, like, through the brambles and gorse, but no one was there, or had been for years going by the state of the undergrowth. So I went back down the tunnel again to the bottom of that shaft. A grille stops debris from falling on the track, but even so if someone had been tipping stones or anything down you'd expect to find traces on the track-bed. Yet there was nothing there at all, and from then on I began to feel fearful as well as downright puzzled. Then I began to hear the hymns again: "Abide with me", "Jerusalem", "Rock of Ages", "O God our help" and so on. It was a regular concert, but there

Constructing a deep cutting on the Great Central

was something strange in the voices, despair perhaps, and as the day went on they seemed to grow weaker. Then there were longer gaps between the hymns, when I could hear whisperings and shufflings, and by the time I'd had enough of it, at teatime, it seemed that there was only one voice doing the singing.

'It took all of my courage to go down there again the next morning, but I made it a kind of test to myself, and I wasn't entirely convinced that it wasn't some of my pals from the New Inn playing pranks. Anyway I took three Tilley lamps and a torch with new batteries plus a flask of tea topped up with rum.

'At first it seemed that all the sounds had gone. There were soft scratching noises which could have been made by rats or other small animals, but compared with the previous day all was peaceful. I was swigging my tea and eating sandwiches when the twelve o'clock down passenger went through. I looked straight into the cab as it passed. The fireman was pulling his fire forward and the brilliant glow (to me who had been working for hours in the dim light) dazzled me as the five coaches rushed past. When I closed my eyes the whirligigs of the dazzling swum about for a moment, and remained when I opened them again to the usual murky dark of the tunnel. The patterns before my eyes continued to and fro for a few more seconds, then of a second resolved themselves into a face. This was shocking in itself, but the features on the face made it even more ghastly. It was contorted in agony – a dying man's face, greenish in colour. I could see every detail: the chill sweat that oozed from the pores, the mud that was smeared over it, the tears of pain and desperation that ran down the cheeks, making channels in the dirt. The vision vanished as soon as it had come, and so did I. That was the last visit I ever made there, and I never want to set eyes on it again. I went off sick and sent in my request for a move, not caring whether I lost the job or not, and that's it. You can scoff all you like, but I bet a week's wage none of you would spend a day down Privett, let alone a night.'

In fact none of the company did scoff. Held by the force with which he told his story they remained still and silent when he finished, and even the young ones stared down at the mugs on the table without speaking or exchanging glances.

I realised that my turn had come to speak: 'I've never seen the Privett Ghost, but I have heard him.'

And I told the story of my experiences in that gloomy place. My tale was brief and uneventful compared with Jack's, but the telling of it

A wonderful study of navvies working on the Great Central

relieved my mind of the terror of the experience, and certainly lifted
a burden from his. When I finished he shook me by the hand and said:

'My God, boy, it's good that you've heard it too, though I'm glad for
your sake that you didn't see the face. It was that that did for me. Ever
since my time at Privett it has been impossible to keep it out of my
thoughts. Now I know I'm not going lunatic.'

Later we compared our experiences in detail in a pub. Jack had read
a lot about the world of ghosts since his encounter with the one at
Privett and now had strong views on what should happen.

'It'll have to be exorcised, of course: I'm a Catholic and I've told
Father Ryan of it, though he's still doubtful. Now that you've seen it
too he'll have to do something about it.'

So he dragged me off to see his priest, who turned out to be a kindly,
thoughtful old boy who listened to my story sympathetically. When
I had finished he turned to Jack and said quietly:

'All right, then, I believe that there is something in that tunnel
which does not belong to the world in which we live. The fact that it
sings hymns would seem to indicate that it seeks some kind of solace.
I will have to inform my Bishop, of course, and I think that he will
agree to an exorcism providing I can account for this poor soul being
trapped there. I will undertake inquiries into that, but I must have

your word that you will speak of this to no one else until the ghost is laid.'

We both agreed to this readily enough and I managed to avoid work in the tunnel for the six weeks or so that it took Father Ryan to complete his research. A postcard from Jack told me that this had been successful:

'Father Ryan has found out who the ghost was. He is coming to put it to rest on Saturday evening. I will come too and will tell all. Be at the south end of the tunnel at half past seven.'

I met them at the southern entrance as the last train of the day rattled through on its way to Fareham. Passengers must have wondered at the weird group that we made in the dusk – the priest in his robes, and Jack and myself in old raincoats and boots. I commented to Father Ryan that it was a shame to spoil his working clothes with the soot and mud of the tunnel and offered him my coat, but he would have none of it, saying that it was important that the ghost should realise that every effort was being made to help it, otherwise it might not co-operate making the priest's task much more difficult, even dangerous. He went into the tunnel carrying a small mock-leather case similar to the ones that masons use.

Jack and I followed him into the gloomy hole. I carried an electric lantern which shone a powerful light on the shiny rails ahead, and we walked for about ten minutes before we came to the place where I had been working.

'The ventilation shaft is about twenty yards farther on', I whispered, already fearful of the place and what was about to happen. At least there was no sign of the ghost, but then they are always shy of appearing to those who seek them.

Father Ryan replied in a normal voice, which echoed from the smooth vaulting which formed the cavern:

'You two will stay here. Do not be afraid, the exorcism is quite straightforward and you are unlikely to be confronted with anything unpleasant. I will be about thirty minutes or so.'

Bearing the lantern he made off up the line. We lit a Tilley lamp and watched as his vague silhouetted figure busied with the ritual. We heard muttered words, probably Latin, and saw him light a candle, and put out the lantern.

The performance of the rite was unspectacular. No fiery demons came forth, or ghosts of any sort. Towards the end I thought I heard the sound of a sigh, as though someone had been released from a position that he had held for too long, but that might have just been my fancy. At last the priest began the repacking of his little suitcase, and then made his way back towards us.

'Well, boys, that's all done with. Let's go to the supper you promised me.'

Silently we walked back along the track and made our way to the local inn where we had arranged that food should be ready for us. The priest seemed fatigued by his efforts, but the good food served to us soon revived him. Towards the end of the meal he began fumbling through his pockets and at last came up with a folded piece of paper.

'This', he said, 'is an account of an accident which occurred fifty years ago when your railway line was being constructed. I will give it to you to read in a moment. When I asked my Bishop if I could undertake this exorcism he made two requirements. Firstly I had to be sure that I was in a fit spiritual state to perform the office: secondly I had to try to find out as much about the troubled spirit as was humanly possible. I felt that I had achieved this when I found the report here, quite by chance, in an old volume of newspapers in Winchester Library.'

He passed over the piece of paper to us. The heading at the top of the page read *The Hampshire Telegraph and Naval Chronicle*; the date was Saturday, 28 January 1899. Beneath was the headline 'Meon Railway Disaster' and the following report:

At a late hour on Friday se'nnight an accident occurred on the new Meon Valley Railway at Privett, a fall of earth entombing two men, named James Owen, and Brown. Owen is a married man with two children, and Brown was an Army Reserve man, and the two were working for Messrs. Relf and Son, contractors. They were engaged in a shaft for a tunnel, forty feet deep and twelve feet square, when, without any warning, the sides fell in and buried them. The tunnel is to be 1,096 yards long, and the central shaft, in which Owen and Brown were working, lies immediately behind the church at Privett, and only a short distance from the residence of Mr. W. Nicholson, M.P., at Basing Park. It being a very rough night, only four men turned up at their work, and while Owen and Brown descended the shaft, the other two remained at the top, one being the banksman, who looks after the working of the crane, and the other the engine driver. The unfortunate men in the shaft had only been at the bottom a short time, when the banksman heard cries from below, and, to his horror, discovered that the sides of the shaft had collapsed, burying Owen and Brown. He immediately called out for assistance, and Constable Cray, of the Hants. Constabulary, went to the spot. It was apparent that immediate relief was impossible, owing to the amount of earth which had fallen in, the quantity being estimated at 30 tons. Mr. Stevens, the foreman, lives in one of the specially erected huts near at hand, and he soon started the night-gangs of the other shafts at work on the one which had fallen in, the rescue party being hard at work at a very early hour on Saturday morning. The men were working in four-hour shifts, but owing to the size of the shaft it was not possible to put many at work at one time, and several days were expected to elapse before the men were reached.

Owen was rescued alive on Monday. He was brought to the surface at six o'clock in the morning, having worked his way up towards his rescuers. He was unhurt, but stated that his fellow workman, Brown, died on Saturday.

THE SURVIVOR'S THRILLING STORY

Owen experienced a miraculous escape from death, but he appeared little the worse for his imprisonment of sixty hours, and on reaching the surface was able to walk to his home, a distance of three miles. He states that when the staging in the pit showed signs of giving way, his mate Brown and he got into their bucket at the bottom of the shaft and shouted to the banksman to haul them up. The weather was very boisterous, and he concludes that owing to the high wind their cries were not heard at first by the man at the top of the shaft. Presently the earth began to fall in, carrying away the struts and imprisoning both men at the bottom of the deep pit. The struts fell clear of Owen who remained unhurt under the pile of timber, but unfortunately Brown was jammed fast by the legs, a circumstance which rendered his escape impossible.

When the rescuers reached Owen he had made his way upwards with the aid of a pocket-knife only, cutting through about 25 feet of *debris*. In accomplishing this difficult, painful, and tedious task he cut four planks of wood right through the centre.

Owen states that Brown spoke to him last on Saturday, when he wished him 'good-bye', and said he was dying fast. He asked his comrade to convey a loving message to his sister.

THE SURVIVOR AT THE INQUEST

The County Coroner (Mr. Edgar Goble) held an inquest at Privett on Thursday, touching the death of George Brown, 29.

The survivor gave a thrilling account of his awful experience in the shaft from Friday night until Monday morning, and described the manner in which he worked his way towards the top through tons of earth with the aid of a small penknife.

The Jury returned a verdict of 'Accidental Death', and exonerted every one from blame.

When he saw that both of us had finished reading the story, Father Ryan took back the account from us and commented:

'So there is the reason for your ghost. Poor George Brown was the restless spirit of Privett Tunnel and, if God be pleased, will trouble the likes of you no more. Say a prayer for his soul tonight.'

With this he rose to his feet, bowed his head to us courteously, and bade us good-night. I walked through the tunnel the following day. It had lost its feel of evil and was less chill and unwelcoming. I often worked there after that, and was never again troubled, neither did I ever hear of anyone seeing the ghost of George Brown again, but I always said a prayer for him as I entered the dark portals of the tunnel he had helped to build.

South Kentish Town

by Sir John Betjeman. Broadcast on the Home Service of the BBC, 9 January 1951, and printed here with the author's permission.

This is a story about a very unimportant station on the Underground railway in London. It was devastatingly unimportant. I remember it quite well. It was called 'South Kentish Town' and its entrance was on the Kentish Town Road, a busy street full of shops. Omnibuses and tramcars passed the entrance every minute, but they never stopped. True, there was a notice saying 'STOP HERE IF REQUIRED' outside the station. But no one required, so nothing stopped.

Hardly anyone used the station at all. I should think about three people a day. Every other train on the Underground railway went through without stopping: 'Passing South Kentish Town!' Passengers used Camden Town Station to the south of it, and Kentish Town to the north of it, but South Kentish Town they regarded as an unnecessary interpolation, like a comma in the wrong place in a sentence, or an uncalled-for remark in the middle of an interesting story. When trains stopped at South Kentish Town the passengers were annoyed.

Baker Street Station in 1866

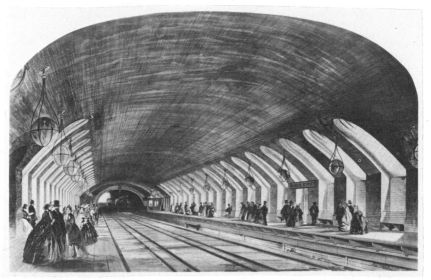

The Trial Trip on the Metropolitan Underground

Poor South Kentish Town. But we need not be very sorry for it. It has its uses. It was a rest-home for tired ticket-collectors who were also lift-men: in those days there were no moving stairways as they had not been invented. 'George,' the Station Master at Leicester Square would say, 'You've been collecting a thousand tickets an hour here for the last six months. You can go and have a rest at South Kentish Town.' And gratefully George went.

Then progress came along, as, alas, it so often does: and progress, as you know, means doing away with anything restful and useless. There was an amalgamation of the Underground railways and progressive officials decided that South Kentish Town should be shut. So the lifts were wheeled out of their gates and taken away by road in lorries. The great black shafts were boarded over at the top; so was the winding spiral staircase up from the Underground station. This staircase had been built in case the lifts went wrong – all old

Underground stations have them. The whole entrance part of the station was turned into shops. All you noticed as you rolled by in a tramcar down the Kentish Town Road was something that looked like an Underground station, but when you looked again it was two shops, a tobacconist's and a coal-merchant's. Down below they switched off the lights on the platforms and in the passages leading to the lifts, and then they left the station to itself. The only way you could know, if you were in an Underground train, that there had ever been a South Kentish Town Station, was that the train made a different noise as it rushed through the dark and empty platform. It went quieter with a sort of swoosh instead of a roar and if you looked out of the window you could see the lights of the carriages reflected in the white tiles of the station wall.

Well now comes the terrible story I have to tell. You must imagine for a moment Mr Basil Green. He was an income tax official who lived in N6, which was what he called that part of London where he and Mrs Green had a house. He worked in Whitehall from where he sent out letters asking for money (with threat of imprisonment if it was not paid). Some of this money he kept himself, but most of it he gave to politicians to spend on progress. Of course it was quite all right, Mr Green writing these threatening letters as people felt they ought to have them. That is democracy. Every weekday morning of his life Mr Green travelled from Kentish Town to the Strand reading the *News Chronicle*. Every weekday evening of his life he travelled back from the Strand to Kentish Town reading the *Evening Standard*. He always caught exactly the same train. He always wore exactly the same sort of black clothes and carried an umbrella. He did not smoke and only drank lime-juice or cocoa. He always sent out exactly the same letters to strangers, demanding money with threats. He had been very pleased when they shut South Kentish Town Station because it shortened his journey home by one stop. And the nice thing about Mr Basil Green was that he loved Mrs Green his wife and was always pleased to come back to her in their little house, where she had a nice hot meal ready for him.

Mr Basil Green was such a methodical man, always doing the same thing every day, that he did not have to look up from his newspaper on the Underground journey. A sort of clock inside his head told him when he had reached the Strand in the morning. The same clock told him he had reached Kentish Town in the evening.

Then one Friday night two extraordinary things happened. First there was a hitch on the line so that the train stopped in the tunnel exactly beside the deserted and empty platform of South Kentish Town Station. Second, the man who worked the automatic doors of the Underground carriages pushed a button and opened them. I suppose he wanted to see what was wrong. Anyhow, Mr Green, his eyes intent on the *Evening Standard*, got up from his seat. The clock in his head said 'First stop after Camden Town, Kentish Town.' Still reading the *Evening Standard* he got up and stepped out of the open door on to what he thought was going to be Kentish Town platform, without looking about him. And before anyone could call Mr Green back, the man at the other end of the train who worked the automatic doors, shut them and the train moved on. Mr Green found himself standing on a totally dark platform, ALONE.

'My hat!' said Mr Green, 'wrong station. No lights? Where am I? This must be *South* Kentish Town. Lordy! I must stop the next train. I'll be at least three minutes late!'

So there in the darkness he waited. Presently he heard the rumble of an oncoming train, so he put his newspaper into his pocket, straightened himself up and waved his umbrella up and down in front of the train.

The train whooshed past without taking any notice and dis-

On the Central Line, c. 1910

appeared into the tunnel towards Kentish Town with a diminishing roar. 'I know,' thought Mr Green, 'my umbrella's black so the driver could not see it. Next time I'll wave my *Evening Standard*. It's white and he'll see that.'

The next train came along. He waved the newspaper, but nothing happened. What was he to do? Six minutes late now. Mrs Green would be getting worried. So he decided to cross through the dark tunnel to the other platform. 'They may be less in a hurry over there', he thought. But he tried to stop two trains and still no one would take any notice of him. 'Quite half an hour late now! Oh dear, this is awful. I know – there must be a staircase out of this empty station. I wish I had a torch. I wish I smoked and had a box of matches. As it is I will have to feel my way.' So carefully he walked along until the light of a passing train showed him an opening off the platform.

In utter darkness he mounted some stairs and, feeling along the shiny tiled walls of the passage at the top of the short flight, came to the spiral staircase of the old emergency exit of South Kentish Town Station. Up and up and up he climbed; up and up and round and round for 294 steps. Then he hit his head a terrific whack. He had bumped it against the floor of one of the shops, and through the boards he could hear the roar of traffic on the Kentish Town Road. Oh how he wished he were out of all this darkness and up in the friendly noisy street. But there seemed to be nobody in the shop above, which was natural as it was the coal-merchant's and there wasn't any coal. He banged at the floorboards with his umbrella with all his might, but he banged in vain, so there was nothing for it but to climb all the way down those 294 steps again. And when he reached the bottom Mr Green heard the trains roaring through the dark station and he felt hopeless.

He decided next to explore the lift shafts. Soon he found them, and there at the top, as though from the bottom of a deep, deep well, was a tiny chink of light. It was shining through the floorboards of the tobacconist's shop. But how was he to reach it?

I don't know whether you know what the lift shafts of London's Underground railways are like. They are enormous – twice as big as this room where I am sitting and round instead of square. All the way round them are iron ledges jutting out about six inches from the iron walls and each ledge is about two feet above the next. A brave man could swing himself on to one of these and climb up hand over hand, if he were sensible enough not to look down and make himself giddy.

By now Mr Basil Green was desperate. He *must* get home to dear

The Safe Arrival,

Mrs Green. That ray of light in the floorboards away up at the top of the shaft was his chance of attracting attention and getting home. So deliberately and calmly he laid down his evening paper and his umbrella at the entrance to the shaft and swung himself on to the bottom ledge. And slowly he began to climb. As he went higher and higher, the rumble of the trains passing through the station hundreds of feet below grew fainter and fainter. He thought he heard once again the friendly noise of traffic up in the Kentish Town Road. Yes, he *did* hear it, for the shop door was, presumably, open. He heard it distinctly and there was the light clear enough. He was nearly there, nearly at the top, but not quite. For just as he was about to knock the floorboard with his knuckles while he held desperately on to the iron ledge with his other hand there was a click and the light went out. Feet above his head trod away from him and a door banged. The noise of the traffic was deadened, and far, far away below him he caught the rumble, now loud and now disappearing, of the distant, heedless trains.

I will not pain you with a description of how Mr Green climbed very slowly down the lift shaft again. You will know how much harder it is to climb down anything than it is to climb up it. All I will tell you is that when he eventually arrived at the bottom, two hours later, he was wet with sweat and he had been sweating as much with fright as with exertion.

And when he did get to the bottom, Mr Green felt for his umbrella and his *Evening Standard* and crawled slowly to the station where he lay down on the dark empty platform. The trains rushed through to Kentish Town as he made a pillow for his head from the newspaper and placed his umbrella by his side. He cried a little with relief that he was at any rate still alive, but mostly with sorrow for thinking of how terribly worried Mrs Green would be. The meal would be cold. She would be thinking he was killed and ringing up the police. 'Oh Violette!' he sobbed, 'Violette!' He pronounced her name Veeohlet because it was a French name though Mrs Green was English. 'Oh Violette! Shall I ever see you again?'

It was now about half past ten at night and the trains were getting fewer and fewer and the empty station seemed emptier and darker so that he almost welcomed the oncoming rumble of those cruel trains which still rushed past. They were at any rate kinder than the dreadful silence in the station when they had gone away and he could imagine huge hairy spiders or reptiles in the dark passages by which he had so vainly tried to make his escape . . .

But all bad things come to an end. After a time there were no more trains. Then, I suppose, the electric current on the line was switched off, though Mr Green did not know this. And presently there were lights in the tunnel and approaching figures carrying hand-lamps. Then a murmur of voices, then the figure of a big man in a boiler-suit, then another. They were the night staff of the railway repairing the lines and testing them ready for the next morning.

'Look 'ere, Bill,' said the first man, lifting up his lamp, 'there's a bloke there a-layin' on the platform. What's 'e think 'e's a doing' of?'

'Silly jigger,' said the other; 'Got out 'ere I suppose.'

''Ere mate! What yer doin' 'ere? You're trespassing you know. This station's been closed for twelve years.'

'I know that,' said Mr Green and he told the men his story. They were sorry for him and they led him up the tunnel to Kentish Town Station. And when he got there, Mr Green, tired as he was, and without even accepting the cup of tea the men offered him, ran up the spiral stairs to the station entrance and went straight to a telephone-box.

'Mountview 6686 – Violette! Violette – Oh darling Violette! It's you. This is Basil. Yes. I'm all right. I'll tell you what happened. Oh yes, I *am* all right. I'll have to walk. Too late for any trains. I was caught in the Underground. I'll tell you about it when I get home. Expect me in a quarter of an hour. I'll run all the way.'

Oh how pleased she was to see him! And how pleased he was to see her! And after that they loved each other more than ever, for it's God's truth that real love, like theirs was, is only strengthened by suffering.

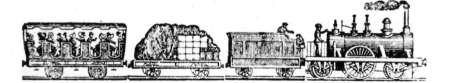

THE PHANTOM TRAIN

When the night is dark and stormy,
   And the clouds are black o'erhead,
When the screech-birds cry in chorus,
   As if mourning for the dead,
When the wild winds are roaring,
   And the air is thick with rain.
Then on such a night, with a shriek of affright,
   Is seen the Phantom Train.

With a roar and a hiss the engine
   Rushes on its phantom road,
With its ghostly phantom driver
   And its grisly phantom load;
And the villagers in their terror
   Cross themselves again and again –
But no one knows how the story goes
   Of the fearsome Phantom Train.

There are whispers of a collision –
   Of a driver who blasphemed the Lord,
And was doomed therefore in this manner
   To suffer ever afterward.
But not one knows the story,
   Tho' the gossips guess in vain –
Yet on stormy nights, with a shriek of fright,
   'Runs the terrible Phantom Train.

Now, who can solve the mystery
   Of this Phantom Train of Fear,
And who can say where it comes from,
   And why does it run each year,
With its headlights flashing brightly,
   And who can ever explain
The skeleton crew, and the driver too,
   Of the fearsome Phantom Train?

ALPHONSE COURLANDER.

Acknowledgments

The author and publishers would like to thank all those who were so helpful in suggesting illustrations for this book. We are especially grateful to Philip Atkins and Sue Underwood of the National Railway Museum.

National Railway Museum, York: Cover, 2, 4, 11, 13, 15, 18, 25, 26, 28, 29, 32, 33 (top), 41, 43, 50, 56, 69, 80, 83, 86, 95, 99, 110, 116, 117, 118, 119, 121, 124, 125, 135, 136, 140.
Norwich Public Library: 3, 24, 33 (bottom), 47, 51, 94, 103, 106, 107, 108, 109.
Leicester Records Office: 36, 88, 90, 128, 130.
The Cambridgeshire Collection: 63, 64, 65, 66.
Lens of Sutton: 20, 31, 77, 124, 133, 136.
David Williams (Severn Valley Railway): 39.
Eastern Daily Press: 105.
National Library of Ireland: 58.